Uptight with the Stones

Crossing Over & Other Tales
Fredi & Shirl & the Kids
An Education in Blood
The Reckoning
Lilo's Diary
Charles Booth's London
  (with Albert Fried)
Ill-At-Ease in Compton
The 28th Day of Elul
The Poorhouse State: The American
  Way of Public Assistance
A Coat for the Tsar

Uptight

with the Stones

A Novelist's Report
by Richard Elman

Charles Scribner's Sons N.Y.

For
Jeff, & Joel & Tony & Dave

Uptight with the Stones

CHAPTER ONE

*I*t was the end of another long day in Fort Worth, Texas, and the sky—like a large pants press—was just about to descend with one hundred or more degrees of freshly steamed dust across the faces of the hundreds of scant, dress-alike children. Denied access to the day's second sell-out concert of The Rolling Stones at the Tarant County Auditorium, home of the Miss Teenage America Contest, they were offering up whole lids of grass, greasy blonde plugs of hash, or perhaps just the seats of their pants, for bootleg tickets. They lay scattered about in a variety of desultory postures on a narrow grassy margin outside that brightly lit flying saucer which looks as if it has been plopped right down into an urban-renewed parking lot, between the void wherein two of the smallest saplings in all of the Southwest separately are wilting.

Twilight, June 24, 1972, and, just a shot away from this

Ethan A. Russell

enormous jived-up Yoyo, a rather big blue and white greyhound sign above the cavernish, square building adjacent to the hall was acquiring distemper.

This section of Fort Worth advertised every manner of restorative for poverty: bail bondsmen, pawnshops, cheapo snacks, work clothes, guns, the Household Finance. It's thirty miles to Dallas by freeway; in transit one passes a large new plasticene amusement park called Six Flags Over Texas, bubble gum-colored factories, the Arlington stadium of the Texas Rangers, rows of brand new toffee-colored brick air-conditioned executive barracks, and the former homestead of Lee Harvey Oswald at Irving.

Halfway to Fort Worth the road was clotted with a viscous traffic jam of Stones enthusiasts. Wild wild horses could not stampede that mob: there were gaudy patchwork knights and their damsels, coveralled sloppies with their ladies, vassals of the House of Clockwork Orange, blonde, duck-tailed faggots and their steads, dealers, young-marrieds, factory workers, going-togethers, bull dykes, fem liberationists, and bombasined babes, as well as studious young swingers from SMU and Hardin Simmons, and every other sort of beefo brawn and banged-up beauty, cutey, and tutti-frutti, bundled together in VW buses, or squatting on giant hogs, or in compact sedans, stickered with the monograms of colleges, universities, reformatories, and schools of embalming and divinity throughout the Great Southwest.

It's Saturday night
And I just got paid,
A fool about my money,
Don't try to save . . .
Gonna rock it up.
Gonna shake it up.
Gonna ball it up.
Gonna rock it up,
and ball tonight . . .

A pick-up full of jouncing farm hands in sombreros was salting the freeway ahead with wads of a dirty grey cotton wool. "Hold on to your hat," my driver said. We moved at last, edging slowly past a collision of the world's largest Cadillac with a covey of smaller cars, my driver cursing wearily under his breath. In between whistling *Galveston* he told me he had three grown "buhs" who loved the Stones.

But when we got in front of that great whited sepulchre he bit down on the steering wheel and muttered more curses about the inextricable toffee pull into which their enthusiasm had forced him for his flat rate fee of $17 plus tip.

The heat was truly scrotum-bloating, pore-enlarging. Like a stack of buckwheat pancakes it fell inertly against the forehead, forcing even the numerous grey Rent-A-Cops to stagger as they sauntered in and out of their contact highs in an atmosphere

thickly *oregenate* with Mexican pot, Peruvian hash, Texas Redhots, and American Nympholepsy.

Have pity for those poor orphans of the road who have found their shelter from sanitized Texas Motel rooms and the hot farting of the prairie in that sallow, tiled underworld of corridors, ramps, and Fallopian tubes constructed chiefly to serve as portals and exitways for America's last remaining generation of tiny teenaged cockteasers. Miss Teenage America my ass. Miss Teenage America was stoned, glazed, and wiggling her ass in the entranceways, on the grass, or the scalding hot tops of parked cars.

There were grunts from the unticketed envious and a perfunctory scramble over credentials when I appeared at the hall's back access gate to demand my press privileges, though, having once entered this echoing domain, I slid, *a posteriori*, all down the line, past sleek black Stones limos, their fifty-ton equipment van, the luggage truck, decompression chambers marked *Stevey Wonder I & II*, and the Stones's personal camper (used for quick-change escapes after every concert)—like a turd on the run—toward the knight with the light from above.

In the first of the two crowded bunkers stood Mick the Jagger, bare-chested and only half dressed. He was smaller and narrower than I had imagined, all slimmed out to a pout, except for some bulgings and flangings here and there, as if he had engorged himself on lemon juice.

With a distracted air he said, "I figured that. Not now Willy later."

A husky man with a face like a manhole cover was being waved out of sight.

Jagger seemed pale. He poked a finger inside his flat-bellied naval, turned it to the right and then back left, as if winding himself up with a key.

He looked embarrassed by all the fuss people were making inside his clean green tile dressing room, as did bassist Bill Wyman, whom I observed next, wrinkling, as if his usually dour face had just been splashed with alum. Wyman seemed to be wearing a fright wig; it was only the slightly mousy page boy of a thirty-five-year-old carefully antiqued dwarf. Underneath the avocado rinse, mildly demure, exhaustion smiled.

To a smallish man in a dirty white tee shirt, Jagger said, "My father has never understood what I do and he never will. I told ya." And then, for a brief instant, all the Stones seemed to rouse themselves from the sleep of rage. They came off the nod and shook themselves out, as in an amyl nitrate rush, and blinked at the crowded air of the dressing room, survivors of the catastrophes of childhood.

Totally wasted, Keith Richards slouched and shrugged and grabbed for the bench under his thighs, and groaned through his little black front tooth, a scarecrow in high yellow lizard boots.

If Keith intended to frighten he succeeded. I glanced away

Uptight

toward angel-faced Mick Taylor who quipped, "Always gymnasiums. Why are they always gyms?"

Jagger pushed between us. There was a second of uncertain cautionless merriment cast across his fawn's face and full-lipped gaze. He was reeling and goose-stepping gently backwards again to avoid the advances of the Princess Lee Radziwill, bedecked with an assortment of expensive cameras.

"I'm sure you must remember Tony," she barked hoarsely, when last heard from.

"*CAN'T SAY I DO!*"

As if warding her off from his thoughts, which were clearly elsewhere, Jagger was like a man wriggling his way out of a sack. There were all sorts of mother wit hip motions and mincing over stated versions of the mother tongue sound that were swallowed up and spat back out again, flirtatiously, as "PLEASED TO MEET YA. EXCUSE ME. NOT NOW LATER . . ." Startled, Bill Wyman glanced up from his game of skill toward his astringently beautiful blonde *frau*, Astrid, and winked, and handed her over $100, his winnings, for safekeeping.

An overhead ventilator coughed out the blues. Somebody took my hand, said "*Pleased to meet ya.*"

Again I heard Jagger's voice: "NOT NOW LATER . . ."

And Wyman was yapping, "Americans never say please, or thank you. Tell me why."

Nobody took up that dare, though, for a brief second of plastic

Ethan A. Russell

time and space, the onlooking faces of the hangers-on and skilled crewmen were all wasted, too, as if smeared with a funny putty.

The Stones have a way of communicating in some pre-verbal manner their own menace: the contempt in which they hold their love of all these American sillies, their love of that contempt, and their contempt for that love. Its sort of a pack look, which Jagger can seem to provoke with even the slightest sniffle or glance; and in the sudden intense silence that in gyms such as this precedes the taking of free throws from the foul line some now were

Uptight

etched like that beside remarkably look-alike versions of wives, old ladies, or new friends of the road.

Tall, saturnine, narrow-shouldered pianist Nicky Hopkins, for example, sat off by himself against a wall, sipping Coke, his face and hair dank, his eyes deep set, while his girl Linda, who wore the floppy bonnet of a Shavian charwoman, chatted with the tour's Jewish accountant about her forthcoming operation.

A Stones PR man slipped a cassette into his hand-held case:

> *"WHERE CAN AH GET MA COCK SUCKED?"*
> *"WHERE CAN AH GET MA ASS FUCKED?"*

Yammer, yowl, and lipfart. Mick's voice complained and wheedled and was cut off sharply with a twang!

"Wrong cassette," a bearded little fellow in a dungaree suit announced. Another cassette was slotted into place, and lo, there was thunder and lightning on the first day, with Dr. John, the Night Tripper.

Jagger has gone off elsewhere, to another dressing room, and the remaining Stones seem unresponsive to the din. They look so cast down, dejected, as if propitiating the God of Worry with a combination of post- and pre-partum blues.

Had they not been among the pioneering firsts to combine the niggerlipping American bakelite of Rockabilly and Delta blues with traditional British smarm, and somehow from out of the froth of this Americanized scum create sensate meerschaum, responsive, prancing, phalloid, a jet-setty fantasy of sounds and motions, a homunculus of Hard Rock enthusiasts to which they were joined, ineluctably, as in an act of coitus? But now they seemed embarrassed for causing such a fuss, for having to live up to such a rep. It had been a dullish afternoon concert, and now the house was jammed again, like a germinating postule, or a lima bean, and would they get off?

At the Winter Garden in San Francisco, it had, apparently, happened for old pro, Bill Graham, of Filmore West and East notoriety, and in Chicago, too (where they had played three gigs at the International Amphitheatre and, in between, with all the bunnies and mommies at Hugh Hefner's mansion), and once in Denver; but there had also been Vancouver, and then the tedious border crossing; Albuquerque, which is like going very far to the Southwest to get hardly anywhere at all; and goddam Seattle, not to mention batting only five hundred, or was it only 333, in L.A.

The Stones could also remember that it had been only two and a half years since they had last toured America when there had transpired the murderous *Putsch* of the Hell's Angels at the Free Concert on the Altamont Speedway,[1] a tour that had grossed out

---

[1]At Altamont, as elsewhere before in America, the most celebrated victim was a Negro with a gun. He was knifed by one or more Hell's Angels. As the recent elections also showed, America's victims rarely change, even after a Rock 'n Roll concert.

large sums from open-air concerts while netting much less, except for bad-mouthing in the press, the hotel bill of groupies, endless law suits, Melvin Belli-sized legal fees (as well as a certain *frisson* of excitement from the psychopathic fringe, and the disaffection of some of their last remaining respectable clienteles).

The 1969 tour stank of blood, of Charlie Manson and his victims; it was the Year of the Fetus, of the Disembowelment. In early summer 1972 the Stones were arriving just in time for the insanity of an election and the attempted assassination of George Wallace; they seemed to wish to appear inconspicuous, and were all certainly a lot less grandiose.

"This is such a violent place. So much brutality," one of their wives kept saying. "We Europeans are just not used to it."

Europeans really get turned on by American violence in that condescending manner in which some parents of 4-H farm children are aroused by the couplings of their kids' prize livestock. The get-off is to go tisk-tisk for shame, and then copy the style, as if to parody it. But this sort of parody has its source in a deeply-felt identification from which one reels with self-loathing. Brecht and Weill fell in love with our gangsters; the Stones admire our bullies, and at the Altamont Free Concert in 1969 they hired them to keep the crowds in line.

It was a set-up for the tisk-tisking that follows mayhem; one spin-off was that the Maysels Brothers hacked up *cinema verité* film, *Gimme Shelter*.

Intended to record and celebrate the flowering of another West Coast Woodstock (and with possibly even more cameramen on duty than at the landings at Tarawa), the film recorded murder and riot, and then was revised via transcontinental phone by Jagger to show his deep-dipped plastic remorse.

True, they had a murder "in the can," as they say in the trade, but there was also much controversy about the opportunism of the new media to provoke such murders and Jagger, who started out the tour as Pan in Uncle Sam drag, must have felt just a bit like that ancient from Greek mythology who ate a mush-mash of his own children, believing his wife was serving him a hamburger.

No matter which way you sliced up the end product, *Gimme Shelter* had to turn out to be as grease-speckled as pure baloney. The Stones came away from it feeling a bit like your sun-ripened Fresno grapes soon after they have learned they are not going to appear anywhere in public again except as raisins.

For the Stones, 1969 was a bummer in other respects, too. It was the year of the late Brian Jones's jealous temper tantrum that ended in suicide after Keith, as if doing a number from an old pop song, "stole" his girl. The year Mick got shot accidentally on the movie set of *Ned Kelly* in Australia. And after Altamont they were all freaking like R. D. Laing heavies.

And, though this tour so far had been relatively free of any serious incidents—due perhaps to the heaviest security for any superstars since Fidel Castro's stay at the Hotel Teresa thirteen

Uptight

years ago, the outward mood was somewhat downish, cautious. Toward newcomers like myself, with possibly a sense of history, they had lacquered themselves off inside a semi-opaque tempera of disapprobation: a look of menace from Keith, or one of Jagger's cold-eyed sneers, and you knew that true Karma meant forgetfulness about 1969. There would be no more freebie concerts on this tour, and less *politique*; no inept volunteers manning scaffolds, or guarding stages. After grossing out many of their contemporaries, the Stones had grown older and wiser: they were now the old pros of Rock'n Roll.

The implication was they had been brought so far down by suffering that all their violent anti-social aberrations had been purged. If I had joined this coven to chronicle a few days in their lives on tour, I had best demonstrate my good intentions by having a poor memory too. 1969 was the Stones's Thermidor; by the summer of 1972 in Fort Worth, Texas, they were trying to pass themselves off as a bunch of middle-class Balzacian businessmen, possibly even with ties to the *ancien regime*, and they had developed this impressive list of nearly forty (and sometimes sixty) British and American professional gaffers, stage hands, light men, luggage men, sound men, body guards, advance men, secretaries, a make-up man, a Production Director, and even a young M.D. to assist them in the deception. It was rumored this might be their last American tour as a group. The last great Rock'n Roll tour, another put-on . . .

13

"They're not at all paranoid," Joe Bergman, a veteran of twelve years with the Stones, told me. "But nowadays they know their own limits. They'll go only so far. You won't catch Mick ever going over the line, and, in fact, he never really has . . . *despite what* the music seems to be saying . . ."

Joe is the Stones's good mother, raven-haired, their black angel. Although no longer an employee, she was cajoled into making this two-month tour on a free-lance basis. Why?

"I won't have to work the rest of the year," she explained.

Joe also provided a bit of testimony about the late Brian Jones, who had been the Stones's original leader until usurped by Jagger and Keith.

"He was a baby. The sort of person who did something offensive to you at three in the afternoon and then called at four in the morning to apologize."

If the Stones have grown up quite a bit since then, they still seemed to feel they needed their mommies with them in Fort Worth. There was not only Joe, but a woman from the West Coast office called Chris, as well as various mommies recruited on the spot to take care of special needs.

One of them told me, "I'd go anywhere in America just to be with the Stones, and I'd do anything . . ."

". . . I only wish," she said, as if sighing, "I could remember where we are and who I'll be going with next."

Uptight

CHAPTER TWO

It was an hour yet before the house lights would go as black as death and the brawny IATSE union light men would flash their spotlight beams upwards, as in London during the Blitz, on a forty-foot-long, eight-paneled mylar mirror that moved on a track, below which Mick and the gang would be reflected as they came charging onto the dragon-serpentine stage. Meantime, there was an hour-long set of blue-note rockbop, the miraculous Stevey Wonder—the tour's second billing—to cool things out; though, from the way Jagger kept bobbing and weaving to avoid the Princess and her traveling companion, a balding blonde stand-in for Peter Lorre named Truman Capote, I felt he must surely know that to be visited at this moment in history less than an hour's drive from the Texas School Book Depository by a representative of one of *that* doomed clan of performers was

Ethan A. Russell

surely just the wrong sort of omen. Mick headed for the showers.

I followed him, after a moment, to peer inside. He was chatting with great animation in a sort of rapid-fire babble of Edward Learish stagecraft and audio jargon with a pleasant-looking, curly-haired English lad in a bush jacket decorated with red plastic STP security badges whom I later learned was Peter Rudge, manager of the British rock group THE WHO, and presently Field Marshall for this thirty-six-city, $4 million sweep through the American and Canadian heartlands that the Stones had dubbed *Exile on Main Street.*

Slightly chilblained with air conditioning under his dark scoop-necked underwear shirt, Jagger had his hands on his hips, and Rudge on his; they almost seemed to be squaring off, except that they were smiling at each other, and were obviously on very friendly terms. Presently Mick said, "Dammit Peter we got to . . ."

And Rudge nodded and bowed, though not in a subservient way, but as if thoughtful, a man with the ability to see to almost anything, and then they put their arms around each other again, and headed out of the bone-dry shower room, when they saw me.

"Who are you?" Rudge asked. "And what do you want?"

"I'm Richard Elman . . ."

"From *Esquire,*" he said. "Not now. Later." He would be saying that again and again during the tour, for he *was* the busiest of men, and Jagger merely smiled at me a little glueily

Ethan A. Russell

and blinked, like a chilled frog, and went out to be among his own crowd again.

"*Fok it!*" I heard him say, after having somehow retreated halfway up the ramp to where roly-poly barrel-chested Leroy Jenkins, Mick's black body guard, a veteran of several Beatles tours, was jiving in blousant white silk tunic and blue flared trousers with three teenaged white girls.

They wore faded backless halters tied across the shoulders with a string, and blue jeans. They had those lovely sort of tulip-bulb asses, lithe, brown, sugary backs, high cheek-bones, and blind, pouting lips, with eyes that frankly acknowledged they were willing to give head under most normal circumstances, but now would possibly consider doing almost anything, including taking it up their keesters, to be at this concert.

"The Stones only come to Texas once every two years." The prettiest of the gang, drawling, stuck her hip out toward Leroy, who claimed to be waiting on some country cousins for whom he had arranged free tickets.

Uptight

"Aw, what you wanta see a bunch of cousins for?" the girl asked seductively.

"Don't fool with me none girls," insisted Leroy. "I can't an' I won't . . .

"Can't promise you nothing but trouble," he added, finally, coldly, almost severely, as he was checking out my Stones access pass for the third time in less than an hour, and then led me back up toward the darkened hall.

Stevey Wonder was just finishing his set; Jagger stood on the steps leading up to the stage clapping his hands, and grooving—a fan just like anybody else. He finger-popped and swayed until the set ended and the lights went up and he edged back into the darkness of a corridor.

A pretty redhead stood all by herself and looked me over, "You're not one of the Stones. You're bald . . ."

"Maybe I've had a lot of experience!"

"Bullshit. . . ."

Leroy sniggered.

The crowd in half-light was keyed up, restless. Some clapped for the Stones. A tall, genial-looking, ginger-haired, ginger-whiskered fellow grinned down at us from the rear of the stage.

As he seemed very sure of himself and what he was doing on stage, I asked Leroy who he was.

"Chipmonck . . ."

"*Where?*"

"Tha's his name mister," Leroy said. "He does light and sound. When he says *hit it* that's when it all happens. Man you never heard of Chipmonck? Gets it all together for the Stones . . .

"Now lookit here," he added. "You can either stand to one side like here, or go back down into the dressing room, and have some'in to eat . . .

"Ain't nobody going to bother you here," he added.

The house was dim, though not yet quite black. Chipmonck breathed into a mike. Promoter Barney Fey's ushers, all rumored to be retired Hell's Angels, stood with their arms folded across their chests at the various barricades which had been erected out of tables on the sides of the big stage area.

You could have cultivated mushroom spores in that atmosphere and then smoked them. One person's features bled into those of another; squinting hard and then forcing the focus was the only way to see.

Gyno-narco is the way I would describe the odor, with perhaps a splash or two from under the armpits, and the sound rose and fell in swells and murmurs, with now and then a hammer thudding, a friend's cry of recognition from some distant part of the hall, or the squealings of feedback. People milled about; others, as if anticipating monalia, sat fastened tightly to their chairs and swilled from bottles of wine or booze.

"*Come on* come on *come on,*" went the piped-in music.

Uptight

Everybody was clapping, lip-farting, rebeeping, and bopping, as if some sixteen thousand bullfrogs had all been suddenly and surreptitiously assembled on the same big lily pad.

Looming above me, mounted in rows of four, like the broadside of a rocket-launching ship of the line, tweeting, whoofing Tichobrae *haut parlers* scratched at the air inside the hall like a procession of crablice.

The stage was littered with Tichobrae casings, huge black and grey boxes and drums for equipment, cables, wires; a greased pole on a hydraulic lift rose and fell and rose again like an oil derrick.

On a scaffolding at the rear of the stage men were sorting lozenges of colored plastic for the spotlights. With my chin touching the surface of the slippery stage I was squinting at a fire-breathing-dragon emblem when another black man, dapper, in sport coat and windsor knotted silk tie, grabbed me with rigor-mortis force by the wrist: "Who the fuck are you?"

"I'm Richard Elman . . . *Esquire* . . ." My wrist ached.

"Well I'm Stan Moore, Security Chief, and you go no further unless I say so." Squeezing me even harder, he led me back down toward the dressing room where a full buffet was spread.

For thirty feet platters of kosher cold cuts and buckets of Colonel Sanders Kentucky Fried Chicken alternate. There are garbage cans full of cold beer and pop, carafes of orange juice, jugs of soft apple cider, a bar mitzvah assortment of whiskey, gin, and tequilla bottles, three empties of Leibfraumilch, plates of

celery, olives, pickles, and fritos, and, as the centerpiece, a large
paper plate of white vitamin Cs, aspirins, alka-seltzers, and long
brown nodules of E that I, at first, take to be the after-dinner
mints. Various members of the official Stones family are bowing
and plucking tidbits from off the sprawl and stuffing them rapidly
into their mouths like those little glass birds that suck colored
water into their beaks which you used to find at all Times Square
novelty stores.

A tall, thin cameraman with gold-rimmed glasses and the
Others have more important business with the Stones. Black
gospel singer Dorothy Norwood, assisted by her choir of three
women, has finished her performance three-quarters of an hour
earlier; now she towels herself by one of the wall lockers and
waits for Martin, the Stones's accountant, to write out a check.

A tall, thin cameraman with gold-rimmed glasses and the
sensitive features of a Henry James traveler sizes me up shyly
through the lens of his Nikon and decides not to snap my
picture.

"That's Ethan Russel," the PR type says; he has a way of
sounding very un-PR-ish and worldly, at least about this little
world, that somehow emphasizes his relationship to the grizzly
chore of publicity even more. His name is Gary Stromberg and in
the Stones's world view he is precisely the living representation of
their under-assistant West Coast promotion man, though he is fond
of handing out business cards pierced, like bagels, with perfectly
empty circles around which swim a sort of text, like the disc of a

22

Ethan A. Russell

Stones concert recorded in a 35 cent amusement park booth.

As a matter of fact, the Rolling Stones's most effective PR arm continues to be the correspondent of the newspaper of that same name, a certain Robert Greenfield, who looks like a youthful Jewish version of the late Buffalo Bill, files copiously, often, uncritically, was quick to inform me that he regarded himself much more as a member and friend of the gang than as a mere writer and that, moreover, he regarded all writing as positively decadent.

It is out of such sour grapes that the mustiest aesthetic stances of a good deal of Rock culture has been sometimes pressed and allowed to ferment. "Go have a snack," PR Gary insists, "a little drink . . . a stick of chicken. Everywhere we go we have Jewish caterers. The food's good here. You look so tired . . . Had a bad trip?"

It's rather nice having my mother with me so early in the assignment. Jagger and the Princess reappear. "*Well of course my husband is Polish.*" She is backing him toward a new corner of the room. "*And they have such different ideas in that respect . . .*"

Heard out of context her words seem to become the context for Mick's next pushing out of his lips. He gives up a fearful pruney glance toward the ceiling, and then an expiring sigh, and they both disappear again, a momentary flash on the history of human psychopathy always threatening never to take place.

Rock such as this is bully boy music; it's the biggest kids on the block trying to act even bigger than they really are—or it's feel sorry for me. I'm Elton John, because I'm a sissy.

The sound of low self-esteem squatting on a Victor motorcycle is the Fifties in a party mask; it is a down hiding out as an up; it's *then* putting on *now* airs; and it can attract every sort of glad-handing freak and creep who can rev himself up for a trendy come-on, and since there is no Rock group that has been

Uptight

consistently as trendy and stylish as the Stones they lose and gain friends with every trendy new album almost as fast as the fly that zips open on one of their recent album covers.

One man's meat can be another's poison. Exactly why Truman Capote has joined the tour in Kansas City I don't know. He is certainly no mere camp follower, and the Stones regard his presence among them with considerable *sang-froid*.

Truman seems to want to have his cake and eat it too. He's brought along two guests; attention should be payed. But everybody has assumed the Princess was, in fact, Mrs. Onassis and none of the Stones seem that impressed with royalty. Over the past decade they've met many a European queen.

Truman looks just as angry about something as I do; perhaps it's the lack of preferential treatment he's receiving.

"That Gary," he suddenly announces, "I really didn't expect to find that sort of New York person on this tour."

Fifteen minutes to go before show time. The writers are interviewing each other. If you catch the eye of a Stone maybe he'll talk to you or maybe he won't. The competition has fiercened. Somebody is shooting a movie in this small dressing room and another fellow is spinning slowly around with a Nagra tape recorder, pointing the mike at the ceiling to catch wild track.

The makeup man has silver sequins stuck to the end of his fingers. He holds them up to the light for the moment so that they glint like a stripper's nipples and then pastes them into the

corners of Jagger's eyes and down in a milk-line *V* between his
sweaty pectorals.

I catch a momentary glance of drummer Charley Watts,
small-chested, too, in satiny red slacks, with his grave, sweet face
bowed by meditation and both his hands clasped tightly in front
of him. The cheeks of his buttocks seem to be pressing so hard
against the slatted wooden wall bench, as if he is just waiting to
exhale once, completely, and evenly before it's time for him to
don a fresh white Stones tee shirt, emblazoned in red with the hot
lips insignia, and thump out the lead for *Brown Sugar*.

Mick Taylor emerges in his fancy butterfly-patterned silk shirt.
Cute and kissy Taylor, his every look a heart-break. When Jagger
stole him away from John Mayall to replace Brian he explained,
"I've had my eye on Mick a long time." He is certainly your
teeny fantasy: a choirboy face and a sourball mouth.

"You doing the advertising tonight Charley?" He points toward
Watts's shirt.

Bashfully, Charley grins, and then fades off, as if he is afraid to
be caught by anybody called Mick looking happy: Again his face
is so wane and his attention fixed to his posture over that bench,
like a shaman to his spot.

"Eat," says Gary. "Don't mind all this. You'll get used to
it . . . ."

He takes me gently by the sore wrist and points me back
toward the buffet.

You can't always get what you want. It's a dope fiend's delight: a little *shmeck* of this or that, nothing substantial. You could get constipated just looking at all that cellophane. Nothing here to produce a solid turd. The toothpicks wear little cellophane dresses.

I grab Colonel Sanders by the bucket and shake hands with one of his drumsticks. I'm carrying on a flirtation with the only black olive in the egg salad. Mouth stuffed with vitamim Es, I wash it all down in tequilla. During the attendant energy rush a special girlfriend of one or more Stones sizes me up as just another *schnorrer* and looks away, bored.

Am I the only person in this room with greed in his heart?

Presently, a few others nearby are seasoning their fists with a white powder which they then hold up to their noses.

What an odd way to sweeten coffee.

"Put some under my lip," says one girl. "Its so much nicer."

She has two very pretty lips on the lower of which is a small herpes spot.

Jagger reappears: "*Where's that Larry? I want my shot . . .*"

"Vitamin supplements," explains Gary somewhat edgily. "Did I tell you we had our own doctor along on this trip? In this and other ways there are number of firsts on this tour. The first tour doctor. The largest mylar mirror. Even what we eat is written into the contracts, down to the pickles. Have something to drink. You look down . . ."

While Gary goes over to chat with a worried little man who is dislodging a large Eclair camera from off his shoulder with a grunt, I think how nice it must be to have your fix any day of the week, by prescription. Doctor's orders, a leaf out of the book of the late Lenny Bruce. Then, of course, if you want to score, you can always take a midnight ramble out on the streets and hustle, like a man who knows he can eat prime filet mignon all week long so on weekends, for sport, he goes out in pursuit of fresh venison.

Presently Gary is standing next to me again. "Its not the way you think it is . . ."

"I'm not trying to think, I'm just trying to look . . ."

A blank look and then Gary is sort of peevish.

"Its probably very confusing to you," he points out. "It's been that way the last few days. They're shooting a film and there are five film crews working the hall . . . plus Robert Frank . . . the fellow I was just talking to . . . who works hand held. Do you know his work?

". . . Anyway," Gary goes on, before I can say how much I admire *My Brother & Me*, and *Pull My Daisy*, "it's anybody's guess how it will all go, but I think they're going to record some of it tonight. You ought to speak to Marshall Chess. That's his department. He's here somewhere . . .

"*O Marshall. . . !*"

Gary is slipping away again in search of the young Princeling

Uptight

of the Chess Records Dynasty, who I am not even too sure I care to meet, and then it's only the Princess and me at the buffet table, and when I glance her way she sniffs at the air, making it clear she has eyes only for Stones.

About then, looking like a grizzled Lincoln Brigader just having made it across the Pyrénées after the Fall of Barcelona, writer Terry Southern enters—seemingly from one of the wall lockers on one side of the room, as if he'd been stuffed inside there the night before and only now just released. He slouches and staggers a bit, and then, immediately, upon squaring his shoulders, begins to sugar his fist, too, and gabs with Robert Frank, of the Lost Brigade, and his assistant, a tall, lean Robert Capa-*Life* photograph of a man who wears the perpetual look of having been hit by a fascist bullet somewhere between the knees and the groin, along with a basque beret.

Mick Taylor raps with the Princess Lee. There are assorted handshakes, sniffles, and snorfels from the cocaine caucus. Truman Capote again appears, flanked by a pretty lad, his photographer, a wild-life man from Kenya. They look like they prefer well-aged Vicks Vaporub for inhaling purposes.

Inside his blue denim Ike jacket, Terry Southern has been hiding awhile, as if lost behind the scraggly growth of his own beard, but now his belly goes abloat and his eyes narrow and he twangs out between blanched tight lips a few lines about his stand-in, Slim Pickins, and the good old days of filming *Barbarella*.

Everybody laughs.

Terry is an excellent mimic. He's a typologist; he tells you who you are and, then, whammo, puts you away. Its a paranoid gambit. Like you're ambitious, or uptight, or a hot shot. That way you never have to know who a person really is, and they never know who you are, either.

It isn't much fun shaking hands with a wall locker and saying "I'm Richard Elman," especially when Terry is doing *shtick* from *Doctor Strangelove, The Cincinnati Kid*," or perhaps *Petticoat Junction*, and cracking up everybody except, again, the Princess.

I turn to her and say, "I guess you don't know I'm Richard Elman . . ."

Snake eyes!

Larry Badgely, M.D., has just passed among us with some of his nifty coral-colored pick-me-ups pills. Take two of these and you can fly to the nearest M & M factory and demand to have your fingernails candy-coated.

Take, Take, so Terry takes, and glances away slyly—a kid with a sweet tooth whose mommy always said don't—and then I take, and everybody takes, and there's such a haunted look on Southern's face when he starts with the Lenny Bruce numbers, the imitations of Stanley Kubrick's dog, his Ringo Starr bit.

30

Wendi Lombardi

Now Terry is doing Yoko Ono, Lord Harlech, the bandit from *Treasure of the Sierra Madre.*

"You mustn't think Truman is prejudiced," the man from Kenya explains to me. "He's just very angry. He didn't come here for the money. Didn't have to make this trip. He had better things to do and besides, he says that Gary's just another little Sammy Glick.

"I'm Richard Esquire . . ."

"O hi." Waxily, Truman shakes my hand.

"Take it easy you guys," says Marcus Welby. "We don't have an unlimited supply of ups . . ."

"Isn't it a pity," Truman says, glancing up at me again, "William Burroughs couldn't make it . . ."

"He may yet," Gary says. "A little later in the tour. Seems the money wasn't right for him . . ."

Capote adds "That's why Terry's here."

I'm wondering why not Jean Genet, or Jorge Luis Borges, or Aleksandr Solzhenitsyn. *Shlock* such as this should be fittingly memorialized.

We're walking up the ramp toward the stage together. In my fist I have another chicken leg. Assisted by three shapely brown women, Stevey Wonder blindly gropes his way aboard a bus. The security men are insecurely tapping out time-step rhythms with their truncheons against the green tile walls. Robert Frank and

Uptight

his sound man, Dan Seymour, rush past. A willowy blonde approaches in flowery silk p.j.s:

"Good afternoon Truman. What time is it?"

"Say, I bet you don't know Richard Elman . . ."

Friendly recognition flashes on her worn spaced face: "Are you the man who wrote that biography of James Joyce?"

"You're thinking of Hunter Thompson. I'm Richard Elman, uptight novelist from New York. My works are numerous, though hardly known at all, east or west of Amsterdam Avenue in Manhattan . . ."

"Mister," says a Fort Worth Texas Sergeant of Police, "I don't know who you think you're talking to, but you'll either have to clear this ramp, or talk to Stanley about a plastic badge."

By now it's total darkness out front and I can see Keith has just emerged from the shower room, after welcoming back a long lost friend with messages from certain of the Tangiers mountebanks.

As if we are all inside this large pressure cooker which has just exploded, a great cheer shakes, rattles, and rocks the hall. A mellow old-time radio announcer vocalizes, "Ladies and Gentlemen, The Rolling Stones," though again it's only Chipmonck.

Racing past me out through the main bull pen onto the stage come Jagger, Taylor, Hopkins, Watts, Richards, Keyes, and Price, followed by their retainers, the press, Security, a few bedraggled women friends, and as the Stones form up in a single wing to the right with Jagger, flanked by those representations of innocence and experience, Taylor and Richards (and Watts slouching over his drums in the full back slot), the spotlights wash all over them with a brilliant, yellowish, sodium glow of white and psylocybin blue, and the audience is hoarse before a single note of music has been struck.

CHAPTER THREE

Over a headset I can hear Chipmonck: "Another ten seconds. They'll hold. They're not quite high enough. *Now . . . Hit it!*" A twang of undifferentiated high frequency feedback blows through the hall. Frisbies arch and phosphor, greenly, toward the ceiling. One plops down on the stage next to Keith's long, corkscrew body, then rolls under the feet of Bill Wyman.

He stands half in darkness. Buddha-like, beyond him, squats big Leroy, clapping: the end man in a minstrel show. With a small tub of rose petals between his legs, he guards Mr. Mick, the Interlocutor.

Chipmonck: "Go white eight. Six and seven up. Pull that amber . . ."

That traveling medicine show of twenty or so plain clothes Narcs, who've been trailing the Stones in relays since Vancouver,

Ethan A. Russell

have settled back into their various muftis, as if all too aware how inappropriate a bust might be at this moment.

Keith's lead guitar stings all the Stones at once so that they begin to scratch at their instruments. Jagger makes a masturbatory swipe at the standing mike, stamps his right foot, and there's music; the audience, pierced through with the brilliant white varnish of the spotlights, has merged to wash all beneath his prancing figure like waves of jellyfish.

"O BROWN SUGAR . . ."

The vast outermost reaches of yeasty darkness in the hall blows a cannabis breath back into my face. It's like gazing into a mouth which has sprung unhinged at the jaws so that it keeps opening up wider and wider to reveal many little tiers of teeth, and one vast palpitating people-tongue, seemingly inert, though pulsing slightly here and there with tremors and waves and convulsions which threaten to vomit back a substance at the focal glitter of the Stones.

A foul mouth, steamy, or patched with streaks of phlegmy light in places, or in other places dark, mysterious, glutted, scrofulous. Tiny microbe people race about the upper tiers on which are refreshment booths, and the little red lights of the motion picture cameras bead the interior aisles like canker inflammations.

Open wider and wider, the harsh initial bars of music display the hip-swaying Jagger and the Stones submitting themselves to a mammoth act of fellatio every time they appear inside an arena when, in fact, it is that sort of submission they are always demanding of their audiences: to blow and be blown and blown again, to the point of vasectomy, or until we all come and can again submit, the degree of frenzy never once relieved by the pitch of orgasm (which is the essential paradox of getting off on Rock'n Roll), as we all go higher and higher, and then, to really reach it and get there, down and dirty, through the creepy-crawly mock-sadism of *Midnight Rambler*, when Jagger beats up the stage with his scarlet sash, and then we are up, off our knees again, with the house lights brightening and everybody freaking through *Johnny Be Good* and *Jumping Jack Flash* and Jagger's theme song, *Streetfighting Man*, as if the Stones are saying getting off is active, never-ending, and there isn't any such thing as release, only motion, and more motion, and *more* and *more* and *more*, and even *more*, until you snap it all shut again, without so much as an encore: and what you're left with then is their nostalgia trip, the good old hard Rock'n Roll days of our childhoods.

All those hands reaching up toward the stage to cop a joint, or touch a cuff? What do they really want?

Even Mick isn't sure he knows.

One thing Jagger is not; he is not James Brown. Never so spontaneous, or alive to his own grace. James Brown, in fact, is not really James Brown, just a carefully schooled and rehearsed

imitation, down to the last finger-popping movement, and Jagger, though certainly a live one, is even more rehearsed, and schooled, and studied in his carefreeness, with somewhat less of a sense of his own body rhythms. For maybe ten minutes he seems to be off and moving. Then you realize he's padding; he's repeating himself. He's just doing the old body-motion time step.

Nowadays Mick is much less swish-my-ass effeminate when he does his numbers; he seems older, decidedly more butch. Whereas once he used to pirouette with a cape on stage, as if doing a hype on his friend, Rudolf Nureyev, as Romeo, now he is into strutting and pouting, with the arm gestures of a middle-eastern carpet merchant, and many a good hard rhythmic stomp.

The mood is less manic and more assured, and Jagger—though much less pretty—seems better organized, like the aging athelete who conserves on each movement to make every one so much the more effective. It was always just a sort of head trip Mick was into, to which his lithe young figure yielded easy assent, the buttocks quivering, though now the marvellous aging effect on the face of the young deity is lubed by runnels, with sweat, the toll from certain putative ecstasies of an earlier provenance, and there is more showmanship and perhaps, for Mick, real feeling, which, of course, is camped up again so that anger seems like the paramount passion and loving is always a function of rage.

That, of course, is an old blues tradition, in and out of the Delta, and when it appears on a stage in the deep South in modern dress in the person of Jagger and the Stones, it invariably has to seem to have the force of high camp.[1] The sentiments hold so well because the audience is locked into the antique moods of their own parents from which they are trying to escape, again, through that musical beat. So what we have then is a very sophisticated double view of things, amplified ambiguities, a highly literate and tasteful attitudinizing of feelings as obscure as childhood which Jagger always stylizes for the crowd.

If some Martian were to come to a Stones concert somewhere in Middle America and be told that what he was hearing was a group of deracinated Englishmen asserting their identities by pretending to be Delta blackmen before a largely redneck audience who, being somewhat in rebellion against their own culturally-enforced identities, are into pretending they are hip international freaks so that they can somehow relate better to that part of themselves which has been living cheek by jowl with black culture for three centuries and largely ignoring it, he would surely wonder if this was an act of cultural synthesis, or just some entirely synthetic put-on.

It's not about relating; it's a glance backward; it's moments of intimacy frozen in time.

[1]For a learned and brillant discussion of how jazz has also been into self-parody, almost from its origins, see "The Duality of Bygone Jazz," by Max Margulis, *The Massachusetts Review*, vol. 2, no. 3 (Spring 1961), 385–410.

The Stones call what they do a fantasy about America. Each performance is contrived to resemble your old time Chuck Berry jam session, or concert, when they are, in fact, highly contrived shows. Sometimes Jagger leads with his voice or his body or a stomp of his heel to bring on the rush; sometimes, as in *Happy*, Keith Richards's lead guitar work is so entirely musicianly, in this context, that it signifies a new mood, a new number.

With his long, crooked body sprouting out of the spotlight puddles, Richards seemed to be some figure out of Jagger's nightmares, an evil *doppelganger* or brother to whom he always deferred willingly for the sounds that mere energy and intelligence could not supply; the two seemed to be working in a tandem, as negative and positive space, with nearly everybody, except for banger Charley Watts, out of the large white circles of the spotlights, though they were musically as much in evidence as the vertebrae of a bluefish.

Stones music is spaced-out. In order to perform it you not only have to be aware of everybody all at once but never anybody in particular. You also have to manipulate an undifferentiated multitude into believing they are hip, *with-it*—the few who have been assembled from far and wide to join hands in rage and flash only on you.

The problem the Stones face every time they perform in public is that they cannot usually hear themselves, much less each other; they must be rehearsed to make certain they are always in some

Dagmar

relationship to what the others are doing, and that all of this is
on cue with the lighting.

It's as if they've all been soldered into their places, with little
moments of improvisational overlap, like the snagging zig-zag
trackings of silver on the back of a transistor radio, and one
movement from Jagger, who has Chipmonck in eye contact, is

enough to make them all flash at once to this or that rhythm.

The way they respond to the vibes of any given hall is to anticipate and manipulate them deliberately. The task is to simulate the atmosphere of a funky London underground club in a hall that seats thousands, and nobody, even close relatives and friends, is allowed to get in the way for even a second, or he is evicted from the playing area.

This sort of role-playing, through which Mick and his gang stumble on moments of spontaneous reality—as if they've been tripped by some length of cable underfoot—requires intense concentration. They concentrate to avoid the actual reality transpiring in the hall, to subvert it, or manipulate it, or direct it back at the hall with sounds and lights and noises.

The constantly made analogy to Albert Speer's Nuremberg rallies of the Thirties is accurate in one sense; it's not so much a question of ideology as of stagecraft, of somehow seeming to be leading an avant garde for millions. There are, sometimes, moments when ideology and stagecraft seem to be but different facets of the same glittery gimmick.

Among the multitudes at every Stones Concert are two or three, or ten or twenty, or maybe a hundred, timid little people who are having trouble getting off to the beat and the sound, the heat and the noise. Either they are too far up front, or too squeezed in tight, too depressed, angry, resigned, envious, aware, afraid, or unspaced, but there they are, anyhow, male or female, the lame and the halt, the unblessed meek, surrounded by their frantic role-playing peers dunking themselves in and out of the sound like half-gnawed sugar rolls and only occasionally enjoying it, too.

They are not so much bored to death here as they are bored to death everywhere, just too aware of the taste in their mouths, or the smelly sweating of their neighbors, or that somebody is jouncing up and down on one of their small toes, or that Lucy Gordon, whom I haven't seen since Third Grade, has become such a really crazy person.

That evening in Fort Worth I noticed a mousey blonde in the front row. She was the sort of girl who dates the goopiest boy in town out of pity and is always coming on to the captain of the football team as if she were his mother. Always inferring you-have-only-to-relate-to-me-to-be-a-much-nicer-person. She wore big goggle glasses and, of course, the uniform backless halter and jeans, yet she wasn't really into any of it, whereas nearly everybody else seemed to be, or were, and it was making her cross to see so many of her classmates up on their feet in growing clumps and knots, clapping their hands above their heads, or swaying, or screaming, or just getting happy, or trying to get that way, and she kept giving off fearful reproaches at Jagger for being such a show-off.

It was as if she kept saying, "I'm a good girl. Don't force me to do anything like that . . . I don't want to do," while stealing

Uptight

44

Dagmar

peaks all the while at that soft accumulated bunching of sexual potency that Jagger, with his hands placed squarely on his hips, flouts like a sporan.

Mick grabbed the microphone with one hand, like a shilelagh, at about mid-length, prancing all around it, like a leprechaun, his face all powdered and silver-sequinned in the corners of his eyes. He was wearing a purple silk jockey cap, a blue denim jacket over his purple perforated velvet jump suit, a scarlet sash, and what you would have to call white soccer boots; and he bowed and scraped and gesticulated toward the front rows, scolding, wheedling, cajoling, pleading; and the truth was he couldn't ever quite get it on with this girl, who in some way became the focus and seemed to symbolize everybody in the crowd, especially his mother.

"*O Brown Sugar*," howled Mick, like a plucked goose, but there was always that girl, timidly untouched by any of it, in the front row center, peering up at him goggle-eyed: *Reproach Reproach* . . .

The bass and rhythm men ran louder and faster:

> *WOP BOP A LOO BOP*
> GOTTA GET
> WANTA GET
> MUST GET
> *WILL GET . . . WOP BOP*
> *GOTTA GET/WOP BOP*
> WANTA GET
> MUST GET
> *O WOP BOP A LOO BOP*

Strung out on the sad-eyed face of this one timid little gosling, Big Mother Goose Jagger had either to call for her immediate execution, or get a fix on his own dancing feet, or else he simply couldn't make it come alive anymore. Not this way: it was like being asked to jack off in front of your own kid sister.

Through the sprung-alive opening bars of *Happy* and then slowing down to blues with Jagger in *Love in Vain*, swearing he "went down to the *staychun*," the mood remained a hype, somewhat contrary and off, as if a speeding troika never quite could make contact with the road rushing by underfoot.

The noises hemorrhaged as ultra-high frequency feedback. The Stones seemed to be in danger either of nose bleed or the bends. They were having more trouble than usual keeping track of each other, and Production Director Chipmonck, who could overhear all eight tracks on his headset, was looking somewhat miffed.

"Its *Midnight Rambler* everytime, you'll see," whispered Truman Capote, from tiptoes, on an equipment box, into a space somewhere below my ear, "they really get the kids off on that one. I don't know why. It's rather cruel I think . . ."

Except for *Gimme Shelter*, Jagger had hardly stopped for as much as an ad-lib; his pace was breathy, like a man in trouble, on the lam. Now the mood softened perceptibly, and seemed to slow. Tall in his ten gallon hat, Arkansan Newman Jones arrived on stage like a Texas Ranger, just in the nick of time, with two acoustic guitars for Keith and Taylor, and Mick was mouthing his harmonica. A momentary warble, followed by a timid request for people to clap and sway. *Sweet Virginia* took the hall with a stomp and a lilt, the carrot and the stick, the sound level was brought considerably down so that the beat could be made more emphatic and simple; a saxophone honked, and somehow that got it together for the Stones and all their fans—the feeling of being close on to the same old simple funky truism burgeoned.

The sentimental self-deprecating hype went from Jagger to Richards to the boys in the band and then spilled into the hall until we were all into it, and Mick was out there, lilting and swaying for the crowds, a regular old shit kicker, this gut-bucket, owl-eyed boy from the Smokies of Great Britain, with his Texas buddies Keyes and Price on brass, so that even Miss Moffet, of the timid eyes and sensual lower lip, was finding it hard to keep straight. She had her arm around her old man's waist and was also swaying and smiling, and almost happy, too, her face unlined by a single fret now except, perhaps, what to do about the fact that she still really wasn't into fucking when they finally got home after the concert.

Solemn as a deacon, Charley Watts flicked away at the sticks. Mick and the boys urged Sweet Virginia to "come on come on back . . . I hear you call . . ." Even Dorothy Norwood was clapping in the darkness next to me.

An elegant brown figure in a derby with perfectly honed mulatto features had ascended to the bandstand, a riding crop in her hand. She began to tap out a beat with the crop against her palm. Out of Nicaragua via London, or France, this was Bianca Jagger; a finely pampered face, a lean, sleek, boyish body

48

seemingly untouched by any hints of her recent maternity. She wore a khaki military jacket and trousers with all the manner and style of aged, imported decadence poured through cheesecloth and refined over generations of depravity, with perhaps just a splash of the shy, well-brought-up Jewish girl—to taste.

Jagger smiled broadly. He had begun his nightly slightly tart and flip nasalized ritual of introducing the boys in the band: "Stand up Nicky boy . . . good work Charley me lad . . ." All that nightly come-on put-on *drech* of false comradery that masks their true comradery of liking each other well enough to work well together at rehearsing the stuff and refining the stuff and then extruding the stuff as plastic, and working very hard at working well together, day after day, for twelve years or so, so that the Stones, if nothing else, are the world's greatest Rock'n Roll band because, in effect, they are the last extant, the only surviving group to make the whole trip together over this grizzly last decade.

You felt their isolation; it encircled all of them in a whirl of light and noise. It was like a soreness in the corners of their eyes that made them appear to be in need of coddling, Jagger especially. He always seemed as if just about to cry. Really break down and let loose a *shreck* like a very little kid, and he never really did, and you knew he never would, wouldn't like you seeing him that way, though maybe with his friends he was different, though you doubted that.

The only tender moments I observed were between members of the band. Their wives and girlfriends were mommies and they treated them all accordingly, with distance and contempt, like kids in a schoolyard angry when they are being called home to supper. But they seemed to know each other much too well to put up with anything less than respect, regard, and awareness of each other's needs. They shared in an attitude that one notes in convicts or reform school boys.

"We're all in this together," would be one way of putting it. They abused each other openly, though tenderly; were timid, even when teasing; played their share of sadistic practical jokes, but hung out together on the road more than one might expect them to.

It was the attitude of waders under whose feet the flushing from a large cesspool is just passing. Always they seemed to be assuring each other that they would dry off well between their toes when they were all on the other shore together again.

"We each have our own lives," Charley Watts kept saying.

Somewhere over Alabama a few days later, Charley told me, "We tour so we can have the experience in common to make music together. The other groups they just stopped playing together, and you saw what happened . . ."

And in Nashville a Stones's friend, who had been with them last summer at Keith's place in the South of France, said *Sweet*

Uptight

Virginia was rehearsed so many times, again and again and again, for good measure, and then again and again and again, again, and then again; and you can't really do that—no matter how much bread they offer you—unless you like and respect your partners. For the sake of the show Jagger was now stylizing all this. It was but another effect, another calculated piece of mood and it, too, had to be dipped in plastic to be made palpable for the crowd.

"Bill Wyman on bass," went Mick. "Take a bow young fella," which was a reference to his bassist's seniority; and then the spotlights washed all seven Stones a fresh, bright-menstrual flush of red, and the *boppity twapippitty* boppity-bopping recommenced as we entered the central agon of the drama—*Midnight Rambler* —and the crowd took off with the Stones and flew.

"Told ya so," Capote smiled; the house was all standees, clapping hands over heads.

It was easy riding for Mick and the rest all through to the end of the set. The last number was played with the house lights glaring and Jagger leaping up and down strewing rose petals on everybody out of Leroy's big tub, and the mylar mirrors tilted so as to flash upon the audience, with everybody standing up and

Jeff Perkell

freaking in unison, and then Mick said "Thank you," for the boys and they raced off as rapidly as they had entered onto the waiting camper without so much as an encore to be driven back out through thirty miles of dark freeway again to the Hyatt House in Dallas.

They left behind a bunch of angry old ladies, the great open maw of the hall smelling of fresh come and Lavoris, and the exits were all kept closed just long enough for the Stones to make their getaway, and the crowd, roaring in ignorance for more and more, were still not aware that the Stones had already split. They came stumbling outside into darkly anal heat, an anthracite Fort Worth evening, with that slightly melancholic cast to their features which all animals wear, one is told, as an aftermath to coitus.

It had happened for them, or almost, *here*—as close as that burning sensation between their thighs and knees, though now it was sort of like they'd been fucked fast and hard in a gang-bang by some case-hardened psychos, at a garden party which they'd gone to a lot of trouble fixing and then had been withdrawn from, and, somehow, they were all still open-legged and supine, in the midst of the fantasy, only without a partner. They were off only

Uptight

so far, with a slight headache, back here in Fort Worth, with the same possessive boyfriends or old ladies, the same boring schools, and jobs, and families, menstrual cramps, or cystitis, and goddamn, Jagger hadn't once reached out to me personally. It was just another show. Why hadn't he sung any of his oldies? *Satisfaction*? Or *Wild Horses*? Or *Salt of the Earth*? Why so much ticky-tock Hard Rock? And for $6.50 why no encores? And maybe I don't want to spend the night with you, babe, either, but it's 230 miles to San Antonio and how else am I ever going to get back home?

I groped my way aboard the Stones bus in darkness, among the crew, the photographers, PR Gary, and the rest of the press, and plopped myself down next to one of the secretaries, and as the overhead ramps were flung back and we edged out into the night among all those angry envious onlooking faces, blacked right out.

The next thing I knew we were in front of the Hyatt House. Charley and Mick Taylor, along with some of the crew, were wandering about with slightly addled looks in front of a large fountain that seemed to have been constructed out of alternating layers of Saran Wrap and halvah.

A groupy walked a largish hound dog on a leash so small she had to bend all the way over like a hunchback and still it hobbled her gait.

Charley Watts smiled, somewhat downcast.

"Get some sleep Richard," he said, "it's going to be even hotter in Houston. We'll talk another time."

I felt as if I had come down among the humanoids again.

Upstairs in my room I turn on color TV. *The Jane Froman Story*. Susan Hayward is standing on a pair of crutches in a French garden before a group of World War II wounded GI's. Abruptly Susan asks, "Is anybody here from Texas?"

Out of the crowd of crippled and maimed rise four perfectly healthy-looking galoots.

"We are Miss Froman."

Then Susan starts to sing:

> "The stars at night
> are big and bright
> (clap clap clap clap)
> deep in the heart of Texas . . ."

and Susan can't clap because she's on crutches but these four big Texans can, and pretty soon even the quadruple amputees are banging their stumps to the clap-clap-clap-clap and I flash back to the Tarant County Auditorium, and then I know Mick Jagger is a very wise man.

He knows that when all else fails with Texans they'll always cop to a good old fashioned sing-a-long.

Uptight

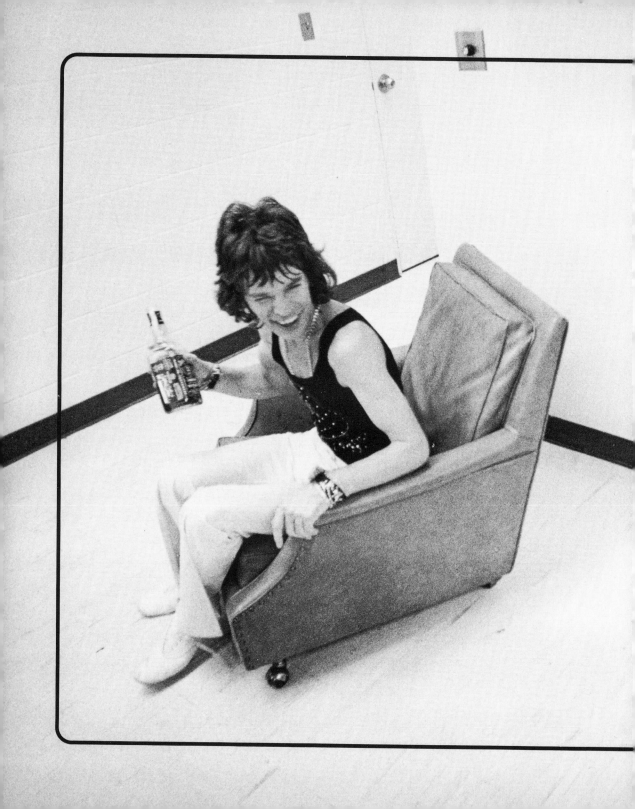

CHAPTER FOUR

It was one hundred and three degrees in Houston, a heat that is to the warmth of Dallas like your Coney Island Turkish bath is to your Finnish sauna. Even when skies are azure in Houston the air is heavy. It is a vast, low, modernistic delirium of a city, lit at night by petroleum crackers. You go from terminal to terminal at the new Intercontinental Airport by rubber-wheeled subway, and there is a Ramada Inn abutting almost every freeway.

Some of the Stones's entourage had planned to squander their $15-per-diems overnight at the Ramada near the Gulf Freeway, when I checked in to the sound of "Ruby Tuesday" on muzak and no swallow-tail-coated coachman in scarlet knickers and green frock coat came out to greet me, I dumped my things and walked half a mile through the scorch to the Hoffheinz Pavilion on the University of Houston campus.

A quartet of middle-aged academics in whites with green eye shades were volleying, in a leisurely manner, on some unshaded courts adjacent to the hall.

In the Stones dressing room, barricaded behind two portable basketball rigs, Jagger bent over a bare sink and splashed water across his face, and stared into a mirror and opened his mouth and went *ah*.

He was wearing an open silk-striped shirt. He unhinged his mouth again like a pit viper and sprayed at his throat with an atomizer. Dr. Larry Badgely asked how his throat felt.

"Sort of pinkish . . ."

Did Mick want him to have a look?

Spritz! *Spritz*!

Not now! Later! He'd simply have to get some rest.

Peering at them from around a corner, photographer Anny Leiberman snapped another picture.

On hand for this afternoon's concert were the same gang as yesterday, with the addition of some local celebrities and musicians and well-wishers: a man in a white suit and a panama hat with a fiercely mustached face like that of Mark Twain; a sharp-featured girl from one of the border states who hung around in hopes of selling the Stones an antique Strato guitar.

The morning after, in Dallas, the Princess had departed to go back home to New York by her own means when the Stones made it clear to her and me and others there was insufficient space for us on the chartered McCullough Airlines jet, *The Lapping Tongue*, with its hot lips emblem painted onto the tail. Told I would eventually be getting aboard the *Tongue* somewhere between here and Nashville, which was only three or four gigs away, I had come on to Houston by public transportation.

Another opening, another buffet. This time with Mexican glop on a hot plate, and three or four pretty hostesses.

I bumped into Charley Watts.

As a very young man, fresh out of art school, he had written and illustrated a little picture book about the life of Charley Parker. I asked how I could get a hold of a copy.[1]

"I'll have to send you one," Watts, with eyes downcast, reported. "Give me your address and I'll have one sent. Not now, later. . . .

". . . Understand," he went on, as if grateful though worried

---

[1]Charley's *Lament for a High Flying Bird,* like other material from the Stones' repertoire, is about loneliness and despair. The saxophonist is seen as the consummate artist because he was different than all the other little birds in the flock, could fly higher, and, of course, had to cut himself from them and eventually come down with a thud—dead.

It's the insistence on death as a romantic fate, on early death, on the inevitability of death (if one truly tries to do one's thing) that is so noteworthy. The little picture book, in tones of brown and yellow, is a simple fable heavy with message: You can't *ever* get what you want!

After a concert in Nashville I examined one of Charley's drum sticks abandoned on the bandstand. It was so badly beaten and bruised and scarred from end to end, except perhaps, for its plastic tip, it is a wonder it had not broken completely into two parts. To see Charley brooding over his set of traps made me sad. I have sometimes experienced a sort of fulfillment through activities such as writing.

about my interest, "I was a very young man then. Just out of art
school . . . and it's a rather naive little book, I suppose, though
I'm not ashamed of it . . ."

Whoever said he should be?

I told him I would really like to see the book, and Charley
smiled, as if somewhat relieved that my intentions were, in fact,
simple curiosity.

Charley is thirty-one, very self-conscious, a wan, thoughtful sort
of person, a worrier, who seems almost dumbly demure compared
to the other Stones but is, in fact, one of their more articulate
spokesmen. Later he *would* sign his copy of *Lament for a High
Flying Bird* simply, "to Richard, Thanks, Love," and I could
believe him. Now, greeting me in his dressing room in Houston
with a faint flickering smile, he agreed to sit with me and talk,
briefly, before the concert.

"Are you sure you want to read my book?" he asked, again,
blinking at me ever-so-slightly, and when I assured him I did, he
said "All those guys like Parker, and Prez. I was a jazz buff. I
used to love them. I still do. They were great artists. Fantastic!"
He stretched out the word for emphasis. "But we're not like that.
We're not artists. I mean most of the time we're not except
sometimes when we're playing together and it seems like we
are . . ."

Charley's accent was becoming more emphatic. He seemed just
a little flustered by the candor of his own perception and glanced

over at me as if to hypothesize how I was really feeling about the Stones.

"Put it this way," he suddenly added, popping an olive into his mouth, and his voice shrilled momentarily and then was almost a glum whisper, "as bad as we are we're professionals, don't you know, every one of us, we're professionals at it, at badness, you might say," he insisted sullenly. "That's the difference between us and all these other groups, and even though we know we're not doing what people like Parker did it sometimes gives us the feeling, when we're really off, that we are. We have something going on like that between all of us."

I could feel his isolation, now, too. Charley has some love in him. He is a man who feels he knows more than he can express with just a set of drums. Closing his eyes he got up, and slunk away from me again. He wants to be his own man and he is not always sure he can be.

Bill Wyman opposite me rolled a butt composed of the makings from a filter cigarette and some tiny, bright green particles that he peppered into the wrapper in a somewhat parsimonious manner and gave me a come-hither look, as if prepared to offer up the narcotic competition of his own ego to Charley's momentary candor; Jagger appeared with his Super 8 movie camera. He panned around the crowd, pointed it at Bianca, poked at the space between them, and then panned some more, letting fly occasional bursts with his trigger finger.

Somebody said, "Jean Luc Godard . . ."

"Gimme Shelter please," went Terry Southern, hiding behind his fingers, playfully.

Anny Leiberman went, "Mick can be very playful sometimes . . ."

I asked, "What sort of person is Bianca?"

The anger was flat out in Anny's voice: "A spoiled brat, just like you'd expect her to be . . ."

Ten minutes later: In a little alcove, Newman Jones tunes one guitar after the next with his antique brown oscillator, a sort of brownish, detonatorish box.

I'm talking to this friend of Keith's from North Africa. He's telling me how nice it is to live all alone in the Sahara desert.

"Isn't it lonely?"

"Yeah man, not really. The local chief was going to give me his thirteen-year-old daughter. A beauty. That's considered an honor. The people aren't as depressed as in America," he insists. "And steak is cheap and good, and only a dollar a pound."

"But what do you do all day?"

"Nothing!"

"Nothing?"

"I'm in the import-export line," he explains and walks away from me abruptly.

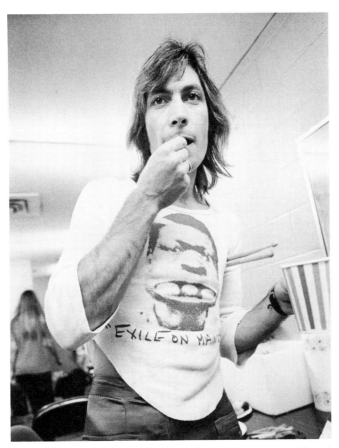

Ethan A. Russell

Uptight

Bianca Jagger has her elegant trousers half rolled down across the swelling S-bulge of her backside to receive one of Dr. Larry's vitamin C injections; the other Stones women are queuing up behind her. Terry Southern glares at them.

Abruptly Keith explodes into view; his features twisted into curses. *"That Stevey's a bloody cunt . . . !"*

"What's the matter now?" asks Charley, looking up with another blink.

Keith says, "Its Stevey Wonder. He can't make it. He just called Mick from Dallas. He won't be here this afternoon and probably not this evening. It's his drummer. Had a nervous breakdown . . ."

"Just what does that mean?" asks Bill, looking up with disdain and disbelief.

Jagger rushes into sight, his arms and legs flailing. He kicks out at one of the wall lockers. "That Stevey . . . that bastard. Expects me to believe that shit . . ."

"What's that about his drummer?" asks Taylor contemptuously.

"You know," Keith sneers, "they probably had a big night partying. You know . . ."

"Goddamn him," says Jagger, his face blanched all white. He stamps his feet. The veins in his face reticulate and he seems somehow to become translucent so that you can see this very angry little person jumping up and down inside his tight tubular body.

From upstairs in the hall one can hear Dorothy Norwood clapping out *The Saints Go Marching In.*

And Keith screams out, "FUCK THAT STEVEY CUNT. . . . HE'S A CUNT," and then Mick turns sober and grabs him and holds him close, and suddenly Peter Rudge appears, and for a second the atmosphere is as hard as cymbals crashing.

Next to me, Ethan Russel says, "Mick's really pissed," and clicks off a photo of the scene.

"Say what you will about these guys," PR Gary declares, *sotto voce,* "they never miss a date. That's the one unforgivable sin in this business . . ."

Mick says, "If he doesn't make it tonight he's finished. He's through. No more jive . . ."

"Fucking Stevey . . ."

"He's a cunt," Keith insists.

Again and again he swears. "He's a cunt. He could get another drummer. Fly one down from New York in a couple of hours. Besides it's a big band and he's got bongos . . ."

Mick starts to kick out at another wall locker but notices all of us watching him and he says, "Come on band. Not here . . . Lets get it together. This way please," and with Peter Rudge helping him to restrain Keith and nudge the others along they go off together into a small private dressing room to confer.

64

With the room so swiftly emptied of Stones there is a vacant, anxious look on the faces of all the hangers-on. People immediately begin to badmouth Stevey Wonder. The crewmen say he bombed out in that impromptu jazz session with Jagger in Chicago; the cocaine caucus find fault with his performances throughout the tour. He's a ripoff, a *pascudniak,* a jiveass charity case. Why he can't hold a candle to Arthur Prysock, or Ivory Joe Hunter, or the late King Curtis.

Still acting like he's twelve years old.

The implication was Stevey had been around the Rock scene much too long to pull a number like this. Ought to know better. If he was being eaten alive with envy for having only second billing, or was in a rage over touring the White South by bus, without proper promotion or publicity, like the nigger in the woodpile, while the Stones flew everywhere in style on their $150-expense-per-diem, that was too bloody bad. None of the Stones, except for Keith, seemed very interested in socializing with Stevey and his big band after the shows, but there were business-like ways to get out of the arrangement and a replacement could always be found. Two and a half years ago the Stones had toured with Ike and Tina and there'd been no problems. Besides, he was really being paid very well, *n'est ce pas,* and he was into this entirely new thing with his Moog synthesizer and getting really good exposure from the Stones tour. What else did he expect? Equal billing . . .

No way! The Stones had only a few weeks left in America and
they wanted to soak up every minute of it among the alienated
nasties, with lots of grab-ars, and tit-ars, and promotional matter,
recordings, rock *verité* movies, parties with the ultra hip, big
deals, gourmet meals, gropes and feels, a taste of this or that,
though nothing more solid than *camp;* and Stevey was acting like
the upstairs maid just after she'd been had by the lord of the
mansion and then abandoned. He was acting hurt, and pushy,
and sulky. After all, he really was an exile on the main streets of
most American cities, a blind, spade musician. Curious then
who the Stones choose as their models and role validators, and
abandon . . .

Au fond, though, is an attitude that Europeans of the middle
classes have always shown toward their paid servants. The Stones
like to think of themselves as artists, but Jagger is also a
stoned-out businessman-type freak, and right now, rumor had it,
he was on the tube with Stevey in Dallas laying down the law.

Dig the scene.

"Hello Stevey, Mick here, and you better get your ars down
here or we'll put you back in short pants and send you home to
Detroit."

"Sho' 'nuff White eyes!"

"You dig what I'm saying!"

"Mick I'm so stoned feels like I'm blind or something . . ."

"Cut it out you nit wit, and get here, or we're signing up

Uptight

Bullfrog Henry as your replacement soon as we get to New Orleans."

It's a standard gambit of distrustfulness to create expectations in another person which you do not necessarily intend to fulfill. The Stones reserve the right to come on to anybody they take a fancy to, anybody equally trendy, or hot, and also to be unfriendlier than thou. They have very little tolerance of human frailty. They work you up to this Big Hard-on and then let you just stand there with it all sticking out like Molly Bloom's hat rack.

"What a lot of jive," they say. Or, "How lurid!" After they have provoked and manipulated you seductively to believe they will party with you, or share their thoughts, or let you cop their joints. It wasn't only Stevey Wonder; it happened to writers like Capote and Southern. They honestly thought the Stones would turn them on. But, quick as a flash, Mick and the gang were looking elsewhere. They were pissed at Capote for making such a nuisance of himself, and they let it be known that Southern had misbehaved with drugs.

Tisk tisk tisk!

They treated their audiences with similar contempt. When a crowd was naive enough to be enthusiastic Mick called them "country."

"It's really crazy," Robert Frank kept saying. "You go to a big effort to get everybody up for you, and then you use all the force you have to keep them away from you. It's like being untouchable. Going through America in a lucite spaceship."

If you want to catch a Rolling Stone get yourself a still photographer. They just love to have their pictures taken, to have their intensities mirrored and flashed back at them, like flattery. With still photographers they really got it on. No matter what the photographer caught them doing they somehow look glamorous, and they loved to look at photos of themselves, and they usually cooperated by freezing every casual gesture, or moment of intimacy, into their own particular deep brown study, as if they could anticipate the blinkings of the fastest shutters, the moment-sudden flashes.

But there were moments, too, when they were simply just too fatigued to cooperate in this elaborate strobe effect of candor, and that must have been when, for example, Keith felt compelled to punch out that photographer in the customs shed in Rhode Island during the latter part of the tour. There were just moments when they had to fall out and, oddly, they didn't like being seen that way, no matter how much they might feel compelled, later, to dissemble falling out before some eager young still photographer.

With writers like myself, though, they struck a different posture. They were curious, interested, distrustful. How did they know what I was thinking about them? And what I might write? I seemed to be talking and acting pretty straight with them. Wasn't that just another mind-fuck?

Uptight

When, at any moment, you feel that any wrong movement from anybody can bring the whole thing down across your shoulders you are apt to look for a maximum leader, a sort of pillar to prop everything up, and Jagger is like that sometimes—a strut, a prop, hard, able to withstand stress.

Or so he seems, at any rate, on tour. Robert Frank told me it was like standing alongside a railway track and watching a railroad train rush past you to be with the Stones when Jagger was in command. You felt that if you got in the way you would be crushed. "There were incredible scenes," he said, "you never even saw."

True enough, I wasn't always invited. I didn't always ask to be. That was my way of getting friendlier under the circumstances. I thought it would be nice to get to know them all a little bit. But they were distrustful, and they made me even more guarded. That most ordinary form of human intercourse we call talking they claimed they were unable to do in a truly straight way. Sometimes they resembled angry children who believe their parents can't really understand them, and they shut me out, as a sort of parent, to make sure I did not.

In fact, the real parents the Stones had in mind understood them only too well, and were angry with them since birth, if not envious, also, as were some of the other writers whom the Stones met on tour who never got so much admiration, or attention, for their own work. So much of a show of love, in fact. In Los

69

Angeles the Stones were paid $104,000 for one performance, and, in our culture, that's a lot of love, not to mention what Terry Southern usually liked to refer to as "all that tight hot sweet young pussy."

Sometimes the Stones seemed to be taking all their publicity more seriously than at other times, and, at those moments, they appeared to be in the market for a Boswell or an Eckerman—a writer to record their lives and thoughts as pioneers, sappers of a new frontier, to share *aperçus* with them, or brainstorm movies, or orgiastic scenarios. It's a role Terry Southern once aspired to, and it's a measure of the Stones's fecklessness and contempt that he was now considered over the hill and that other writers, including myself, I suppose, were being looked over now as possible candidates.

"When you're hot you're hot," Terry kept saying, "and Richard you're hot."

If Terry ever wins the Nobel Prize it will be for the put-on. He seemed so worried.

The Stones had chanted, *"Time* is on my side," and Terry must have felt he really couldn't be getting that old if he really was able to make it with all these smartass kids.

As I say, it was a really uptight situation. The attitude of the Stones seemed to be if-you-give-me-anything-less-than-complete-flattery-you-are-out-to-do-me-in. Yet there were also those moments when they seemed to wish to be seen, and

Uptight

exposed, were willing to *be* open and available, if only somebody were truly tender with them. It wasn't just a tease, either. They really needed that sort of friendliness—and they knew it—for somebody to hear them out, with their grudge. But would they be prepared to listen, as well, and be helpful, too? If time was truly on their side did they have the time to waste being helpful with others?

I think of Bill Wyman coming over to Charley and me aboard the *Tongue,* again and again. Once he caught us just being quiet together, and he peered down hard, his eyes blazing rage, and, as if boasting, or warning Charley, or both, said, "I told him our real ages . . . told him who we really are," and then sniggered, as if to make a joke of his anxious little freakout, and disappeared again.

As early as *Jig Saw Puzzle* Mick could describe somebody who was strung out as a "walking clothes line." His respect for the power of the word can be ascertained from the kinds of imagery that he spackles into his songs. His lyrics often seem to be a gloss on the modernist *Zeitgeist* of writers from Baudelaire to Burroughs. *Sister Morphine,* for example, is like something out of late nineteenth century French poetry; and *Sympathy for the Devil,* which everybody took to signify Mick's conversion to Satanism, was really just a borrowing from the post-revolutionary

Ethan A. Russell

Uptight

Russian black humor novel, *The Master and Margarita* by Mikhail Bulgakov.

The reader will note that much of Jagger's written entertainment seems to be published by the Grove Press, or its English equivalent. It is a taste that inclines heavily toward self-dramatization and S-M, whether camped up, or written as confession, but one must not necessarily conclude that Mick's reading habits are any indication of his own inclinations. Rather, they would seem to reveal him as an auto-didact from a Puritanical household who felt he had to state love in its extremes to locate any tender erotic feelings whatsoever inside himself.

Throughout the tour Robert Frank complained about how difficult it was to get "something real" out of Jagger.

Jagger's choice to make another Rock movie of the event had been with the tour since Vancouver, at times just barely hanging on. He kept saying it was the hardest job he'd ever taken on. "Its as if they're entirely insulated, wrapped in Saran Wrap," Frank insisted. "I'm intrigued by Mick. He's awfully smart and very capable. I can't help liking him. He's so smart. I'm just having a bad time."

Robert is Swiss-born. Sometimes, if exhausted, a bit of the old accent seeps through. "I like him," he repeated to himself. "I can't help it." It was almost as if he was trying to convince himself. Frank has known many difficult people in his time, like Kerouac, Ginsberg, Corso. He's explored the withdrawal of the schizophrenic, toured the Deep South of tent meetings and the White Citizens Council, and he has some real loving feelings when he is with you over a cup of coffee, or a drink. Something about Jagger's seeming ebullience, his way of coldly manipulating situations, his shrewdness and canniness, was both attractive and repellent to Frank's artistic sense.

He said, "He picks up on everything so fast. Look at the way he learned to use my Super 8 camera. Most people in his position would not even bother. They'd get somebody else to do it for them. All I had to do was explain to Mick how it worked just once, really quickly, too, because I was busy, and there he was. He picks up on things so fast. He's smart, more like a very canny businessman than an artist, if you know what I mean. He's very smart."

Next to us on a hot plate bubbled an ooey-gluey orange mess of burritos. It was that sort of primal ooze out of which it almost seemed, briefly, as if Mick had just emerged through the ministrations of this kindly European scientist, Dr. Frank, as in one of those old movies, after which, of course, the mad Dr. Frank might declare astonished to the point of a catalepsy, that the monster was "truly smart."

I spotted Bianca and Jagger, standing side by side, with their arms around each other. They were hugging and touching hips, and holding each other, closely linked together, a couple of nice young teenagers.

Ethan Russel snapped their photo, too, again, and then again.

"I really do like Mick," Frank insisted then, as if surprised that he could. "He's very intelligent . . ."

"Smart," I said, turning away to ask Dorothy Norwood, who was sipping at a Coke like a plump black little teenybopper, what she thought might have happened to Stevey Wonder.

Dorothy has been "in the business" a long time. She has a tart plum face, and a friendly smile, but there's a little bitterness there, too. Time isn't on her side and she'd like to make it bigger before she passes on and Savoy Records, Newark, New Jersey, can't really do that much for her. So she just has to take the main chance.

Now she was glancing about the room somewhat gravely when her face brightened, as if she were experiencing some pleasant memory.

"You know something," she said, "when I got that telegram from London saying the Stones wanted me I was just so happy. That really was something. Imagine Mick Jagger wanting me. I was happy. Told my agent, what do he want me for? The Rollin' Stones . . ."

The man with the Nagra tape recorder slowly revolved on his heels, his mike pointed up toward the ceiling. In this cruel competition for attention, in which we all got higher and higher he would spin, like a top, for minutes at a time, hoping to catch any stray sounds of significance—a radar scanner, or a divining rod—as if he could geiger counter all the vibes in the room at once.

Dorothy asked, "Why do *you* think they wanted me?"

"I don't know . . . because you're good . . ."

"Uh uh!"

"You're a pro . . ."

"No use worrying about that," she said, and smiled, real big, for Ethan Russel, who then snapped her picture, too.

CHAPTER FIVE

The Houston concert that afternoon was a stand-up explosion of joy and rage from beginning to end and, afterwards, the Stones went off to the Ramada Inn to the suite of Ahmed Ertigan, President of Atlantic Records, for a party.

Ertigan is a medium-sized, chubby, dapper-looking bald man with mustaches, a sloped skull, and a cold glitter to his eyes. He looks a bit like a shrewder, more degenerate version of Esky, and he had come to Houston accompanied by a sinewy black PR man named Mario, and a handsome Amazonian blonde.

He was on his way to Los Angeles, Ertigan explained, and just wanted to stop by to say hello to the Stones, having recently signed this multi-million dollar contract to produce their records through Atlantic.

"I do it with all of our artists," insisted Ertigan. "It's a custom with Jerry Wexler and me in our company. By the way, what's your angle for your story . . . ?"

Ethan A. Russell

Behind a closed door, in another part of the suite, the Stones were resting. A waitress went about the room with a tray of tiny little Texas meatballs. The crowd was sullen, subdued, on couches, or slouching across the floors. One flight below, outside, in twilight, groupies and would-be Stones dope dealers romped in the pool, and splashed, and tried to catch the eye of somebody on the balcony and get invited up to the party.

A one-armed cop barred the stairway up to the suite.

"What do you think your angle will be on the Stones?" Ertigan demanded of me, cautionless for a moment.

I did not have an angle that I knew of so I shrugged and asked how *Exile On Main Street* was doing.

He assured me it was "doing just fabulous."

"And it's a lousy market," he said. "We have a million sales already and you have to remember it's a double album . . .

"You have to remember," Ertigan added, hastily, "they're the Stones . . ."

Keith poked his head out through the door to the other room and demanded to know if Stevey had shown up.

He seemed as glazed as a condemned man waiting to be hung and was called back inside from somebody behind and he obeyed, the door shutting on him just as I heard him say, "Fuck that . . . Fuck the cunt I say . . ."

The rooms above the chlorine-blue motel pool were suddenly quite still.

Again Ertigan asked, "What's your angle?"

And when, with a shrug, I again refused to answer he went

into the other room to be with the Stones, and I was left with Mario of the double-knit polo and tinted glasses.

"What did you say your name was?"

"Just call me Mario. Everybody does."

"What do you do?"

"What do you think your angle will be?" he demanded.

Again I shrugged.

"You don't know?"

"Frankly no . . ."

Mario backed away and sat down with Charley to talk about jazz.

Truman Capote was showing Terry Southern the contents of a large black medicine bag full of ups, downs, trancs, and laxative pills.

I had lent Ethan Russel the key to my room so he could borrow a bathing suit and take a dip in the pool. He came back swearing he felt refreshed.

"That really made a big difference. . . . Thanks . . ."

"Ethan where were you?" Joe Bergman demanded.

The milling about had recommenced. "Come on band. Let's get going. Come on. Act like a band. We have a concert to do."

In a black top hat and silky white slacks, Jagger seemed alert and efficient. As he rounded up everybody and had them stand in a line, for a moment, like school children and he counted off, he bit his lips, and the lines on his face sagged, and then one by one, the Stones trooped after him onto the balcony and down the stairs, into a brace of waiting black limos.

Uptight

CHAPTER SIX

7 he Stones rested for two days in New Orleans, and partied and played a bit, and sacked out and gave no concerts in "that filthy Mafia town," as Keith would later put it.

We saw each other only fleetingly, occasionally. Mostly they kept to themselves, shopped, rambled about in large groups late at night through the French quarter, and tried out some of the more exotic local delicacies. It was their first stay in the birthplace of jazz and they were exceedingly respectful of all the landmarks, just like German tourists at Chartres, and seemed anxious not to defile any sacred texts of jazz history by getting off with their stuff here. Also, no hall was, apparently, adequate to their needs.

On just what little white or black sailed ships they were wafted through the hot gumbo New Orleans days and nights I know not. They came and went their separate ways. Once I spotted Mick

Taylor entering the lobby with something bundled up inside a bath towel. He wore brown and white English schoolboy shoes and looked just a bit like some young sailor who has arrived in port to make a score; and he preferred not to recognize me which was understandable since I had so very little to say to him except to praise his guitar playing which, of course, would have only made him paranoid and defensive to the point of putting himself down again, as he'd done previously.

So it went with Taylor and myself. We were just a generation apart: I still had trouble with his calling and he with mine.

On the evening after we arrived, a second party that lasted through most of the night was given by Ahmed Ertigan at Camp's Jazz City, a recording studio in a slummy section of town. On hand to play for the Stones were a barrel-house Kansas-City-Style pianist and shouter, Roosevelt Sikes; he looked a bit like the late Jimmy Rushing, mummified, and had a similar whiskey tenor sound. There was Professor Longhair, humming the boogiewoogie blues he played; he's the original Dr. John. The great 50's blues guitarist Snooks Eaglin came and stole the show with a two-hour-long virtuoso performance; and he was preceded by a sullen but energetic group of contemporary black jazzmen with a loud linear sound, and by an old-fashioned Dixieland funeral band led by two elderly gentlemen of color, one stout and solemn, the other cadaverous but grinning, both with parasols, who strutted in that close air and had everybody up on their feet, after a while, trucking with them.

It was a fine shimmy of a party; there was a friendly, easy spirit in the room, for the most part, with members of the band paying respectful and close attention to the work of the local musicians who were all being paid to perform, and Mick and Keith and their friends arriving very late and somewhat exhausted, having driven by limousine from Houston so they could do some sightseeing and tripping and bar-crawling with Leroy and Bobby Keyes. In the town of Houma, Louisiana they were asked to leave the Stone Bar because they had brought with them a gentleman of color; and, in general, the trip had been an irritant—hot and tedious—so that they seemed a bit out of sorts when they finally arrived, late, for the party.

Feeling exhilarated by the music and the jambalaya of friendly women on hand, I went over to greet Jagger; he was really not in a very talkative mood.

"Looks like you didn't have much fun."

Mick agreed that he had not.

"Why did you do it in all this heat?"

"Because I hadn't ever done it before," he explained, crossly, almost petulantly.

Later, when he saw me dancing and getting off with a pretty local girl, Mick's attitude softened. Leaning against one wall with Bianca, he smiled benignly at everybody: the musicians, the dancers, his friends, and guests, as if his only delight at the moment was to vicariously observe the pleasure of others. He

Uptight

seemed locked into his disagreeable mood of the afternoon, and he looked just a bit lonely, too.

Mick stayed only a little while and then, at Bianca's urging, split.

Early the next afternoon a Stones PR man invited me to his room to tell me I had a seat on the plane.

We smoked and he played his cassette for me of *Cocksucker Blues,* as if entirely oblivious to the scene in the dressing room that first day.

"It's a bootleg," he explained. "Mick may do a whole album of obscene songs next year. I wish you wouldn't mention it."

He winked.

I winked back.

Like many of the best Stones songs, *Cocksucker Blues* is a hype on certain working class British social facts. Standing next to Nelson's column in Trafalgar Square a boy from the provinces shouts about his lugubrious loneliness:

> Where can ah get ma cock
> sucked?
> Where can ah get ma
> ass fucked?

I was reminded of the Stones revolutionary hymn *Salt of the Earth,* that International for heads, sung by a chorus of zonked-out freaks, so rich in self-deprecation and self-knowledge.

But, at least, we were getting somewhat closer to home here with *Cocksucker Blues*. Trafalgar Square, I reasoned, was certainly much much closer to where Mick really seemed to live than, say, Houma, Louisiana.

I had another brief flash of spruce Ahmed Ertigan demanding of me, softly, "What's your angle?"

To assume the angle right off, I concluded, was to convince myself that one angle might be preferable to Jagger than, say, any other.

CHAPTER SEVEN

The highest privilege the Stones bestowed on anybody I knew of was to fly with them in the *Tongue,* their chartered plane, sipping tequilla sunrises, and eating from a buffet table of cold cuts and salad fixings that seemed to have been transported right out of one of their dressing rooms by the Twin Caterers of Eastern Parkway, Brooklyn.

It was at such moments that interviews were granted, and there were numerous friendly interchanges between members of the band and the press; people got to know each other just a little bit better.

Charley would ease his tension by doing cartwheels in the aisles.

Usually Mick and Bianca would sit in the front seats, chatting softly, like a patient to his psychiatric nurse, or else

Uptight

Ethan A. Russell

they would be playfully nudging each other, like schoolmates.

In a lounge at the rear of the plane the caucus regularly assembled.

Some people amused themselves by overseeing the work of the pilots in the cockpit. Others gossiped. The photographers snapped their pictures, as if to record any moments of putative spontaneity, and the always-pleasant Peter Rudge and his staff worked and planned from their situation reports on the next leg of the tour, and the next. And the next.

My request for an interview with Jagger was motivated as much by perfunctory zeal as by any clear indication that it was likely to be illuminating, in specific ways. Mostly I simply wanted to carry on a conversation with him so as to get some sense of how his mind worked and, of course, he took the lead right out of my hands and put me away. When you've been interviewed as many times as Mick Jagger it's hard not to take charge and make a show of the matter. Mick was frank, I suppose, though he was never really candid; he answered all my questions, responsively enough, but said as little as possible.

I asked if this was going to be the last American tour.

"Certainly not," Jagger eagerly declared. He told me of his plans to tour the Far East, and also some Eastern European countries, said nothing more about coming back to the States.

In January of this year the Stones toured most of the Far East, including Japan. I was asking Jagger in July, is touring really fun?

Ethan A. Russell

"Of course," he insisted, "and it's a necessity." He sermonized on how difficult it was to play together and write together unless you continued to have experience in common.

I expressed my ignorant belief that all the Stones hung out together in the South of France.

"I can't really hang out anywhere . . . I just can't live anywhere . . . Next year I'm going to try Ireland . . ."

Uptight

Ethan Russel and Anny Leiberman were snapping our pictures. We had reached a pitch of openness which, perhaps because of my own timidity, or Jagger's cockiness, soon got roofed over and closed hermetically about us, like a tarpaulin falling in front of a live performance.

Briefly Mick wondered about me.

Why had I come on this tour?

"Because *I've never done anything like this in my life,*" I explained. "Just like you driving from Houston to New Orleans . . ."

Mick's expression allowed that was plausible, though hardly very interesting, and then I explained that I was a rather timid person, and thought he probably was too, and he looked blankly ahead and did not even respond.

We were seated together in the front seat, crossing above carefully divided acres of hazy green American farm land. I said, "It looks more peaceful than it really is . . ."

Jagger didn't respond.

I asked about his trip to Eastern Europe. "Those people really have nothing," he exploded. "They've been raped. All that Socialist bullshit. They're a bunch of robbers and gangsters over there!" It sounded just like some working-class British fifteen years ago putting down the Labor Party. Socialist Bullshit. That was the key word. I'm making it! Up yours! I'm not taken in by you! I see what sort of milksop you are!

That was Jagger's message. It did not seem to matter what we spoke about. His theme was contempt. He was the Paganini of the put-down.

Again I asked about his future plans. I had heard he wanted to make feature films. "I've bought myself some equipment," Jagger, like an incipient hobbyist, responded, as if shy.

"A little editing block, I suppose, and a moveola . . ."

"Something like that, yeah," Mick said, swallowing his sneer.

"Basically," he added, then, "I'm a performer. That's what I do. Sing . . ."

We talked about some of our favorite vocalists and I told him how much I had once enjoyed the work of black vocalist, Marvin Gay, especially his former duets with the late Tammy Terril.

Mick launched into an accurate and acidic attack on the exploitation of certain black artists by Motown Records, and then inquired if I liked any of Marvin Gay's recent work. He referred specifically to the album containing "Save the Children," entitled *What's Going On?*

I told him I did not.

"Ecological Rock," went Jagger. "Save the world by saving a bunch of tin cans. I don't buy that jive bullshit. All that bullshit isn't Rock'n Roll. It's just good-will jive." And then he smiled at me openly, in a friendly way, said he would now like a cup of tea, nodded, smiled somewhat more secretly again, as if to announce he'd got my number, and went back to join Bianca who

was chatting softly with Terry Southern.

Above all, Mick had wanted me to see that he *was* hip, was protected; he could wade through shit and, no doubt, had, though never again, if he could help it. Jagger has the guile and savvy of a survival artist, and the energy and charm of a young advertising vice president. He will continue to rise, to go farther and farther, if need be. He may have been unhappy but, he is not about to kill himself. He has perfected a certain style for his despair. He's one of those men, in Saul Bellow's words, who knew and knew and knew, or so he might have claimed.

As I returned to my seat I could tell our conversation had attracted the attention of a lot of others on the plane. Having been granted such a special privilege, I was now required to share whatever wisdom I had gleaned, or, at least, own up to the fact that like so many others I'd struck out.

I thought to myself what else can a poor boy do but play rhythm and blues.

Certainly, he would not want to be caught scavenging up tin cans to help save the world.

For Jagger's style is the 50's revisited; it's the cover for *Exile on Main Street;* a nostalgic transformation of teen angel and earth angel as black angel. It's Clarence Bullfrog Henry and Screaming Jay Hawkins with tennis balls stuffed inside their mouths. I think the American South was a disappointment to Mick. He'd have dug it more if, say, people were just a little more up front about

Ethan A. Russell

their feelings, like at a lynching. He'd been brought up in that terror and anxiety of Existential despair fobbing itself off as petty bourgeois respectability and he was just not about to respond to any friendly gestures from a person like myself, a stranger.

Jagger was hip. Man was a predatory beast. He knew. Mick could feel the monster gnawing away at his guts, at his inner lip. He'd seen too much, and done too much himself.

Going back to my seat, I scooped some polyurethane roast beef off the buffet, and ordered myself a double tequilla sunrise.

Robert Frank came and sat down next to me.

"You see what I mean," he observed. "He's very smart, isn't he?"

"He's seen an awful lot go down," the always-respectful Bob Greenfield chimed in, like an Ink Spot.

It seemed somewhat incredible to me that they were using such tones of hushed obsequious reverential awe for an under thirty pop singer who sometimes knows how to shake his ass, as in Eldridge Cleaver's famed prophecy, except that Ethan Russel then came by and snapped a picture of the three of us, chatting together, and that seemed to make it a piece of instantaneous pop history.

Uptight

CHAPTER EIGHT

Stevey Wonder's drummer had, indeed, freaked out. At Mobile the band reappeared with a new drummer and nearly tore the house apart. You could actually feel the floor moving in waves and rumblings under your feet; the limos bounced softly on their rubber tires in the ramps outside the hall, and that only happened once again with the Stones, that I observed, in Madison Square Garden.

It was as if Stevey and his gang were out to prove they could do the Stones in, even from second billing. They were all over the stage, screaming like banshees, blowing fire horns, and cooling out everybody in the hall with the medicinal properties of their drowsy opiate of funk.

Jagger and the Stones weren't listening. They were really dragging ass. I kept running among them to ask, "Are you hearing Stevey Wonder? Dig what he's into tonight. He's clawing

Ethan A. Russell

and scratching and beating up on your audience like they were like a bunch of little white Smith girls with their legs spread."

The Stones were trying to remain cool. They knew their audience, and it was not Stevey Wonder's audience. No matter what he did in that hall, even if he whipped it out and whacked off into his Moog synthesizer, the crowd would wait to come with the Stones. It seems they could get higher just anticipating Mick's entrance than they could by merely grooving on the presently available Stevey, and so they bided their time, and sat, and remained cool. Jazz wasn't their thing; they preferred a lighter shade of plastic.

It was like the way some women are about the men in their lives: this guy may look very promising as a one-night stand but since he isn't what they were promised when they were little girls on their daddies' knees they don't even want to take a chance of letting go. Stevey whirled blindly around on stage: he made sucking and fucking noises; and the sound of his voice slithered in and out of the Tichobraes like a well-practiced cock, yet the crowd remained tight; they were faithful to Jagger and the Stones. They weren't about to come in even some cut-out way for Stevey. They were saving it all for Mick. Finally, Stevey got pissed and lost his high and called it quits and left the stage. He'd just been with the girl who has a drink with you after work but refuses to get turned on because she has a date with her boyfriend later.

Keith Richards was the only Stone waiting around to

congratulate Stevey as he came off. Keith was profuse and abject; he let the band know how right on they were, and then there was much laying on of hands, and numerous "beautifuls" were exchanged. They'd had a little lovers' quarrel but now they were all friends again and that new drummer from Chicago certainly was heavy. They would all have to party sometime later in the tour, perhaps tomorrow night in Tuscaloosa.

For the Stones, Mobile produced the keys to the city, a hall large enough to stage *Peter Pan,* and a house full of neatly trimmed long-haired kids from the neighboring Gulf summer resorts: from New Orleans, Biloxi, Birmingham, and from the tiny little black earth and red clay farm towns nearby where they still use words like "boger."

It's a small city that reeks of petroleum and pollution, with a skyline that resembles a lower jaw with only one or two yellow teeth in place. The crowd seemed as anxious to please the Stones as a bride preparing her first meal at home. They whooped it up from the first note, threw frisbies, exploded green stink bombs, were on their feet long before *Midnight Rambler,* bobbed and weaved slowly with *Love in Vain,* and by the time the Stones were closing on *Streetfighting Man* they had successfully resolved all existing scientific doubts about the possibility of the vaginal, as well as the clitoral, orgasm.

Such abject enthusiasm for a performance in which they had been clearly outflanked by Stevey Wonder seemed to disgruntle

Dagmar

some of the Stones. On *Midnight Rambler* Jagger's movements were so out of synch with the lights and the drama of the music that it was like watching an unsprocketed movie. The usually unchippable Chipmonck screamed into his head set and leaped up and down like a patient under electric shock.

Afterwards Mick Taylor said he felt the Stones had performed poorly, and Jagger remarked they had sounded "a bit too countryish, you know, hick." He seemed to be aware that his spontaneous outbursts of rage in *Midnight Rambler* did not bear up too well under constant repetition, but, like a man with a jagged electrocardiogram when his doctor tells him *stop drinking,* he shrugged off my suggestion that he kill that part of the number.

Mick said, "We have to do it every night. They expect us to."

"I thought we played very well tonight," Nicky Hopkins told me later on the plane, as if in defense of Jagger. He was cooling out. Nicky was always cooling out somewhere in a dark corner with his girl Linda who always seemed to be in agreement with him, as if his timid manner and weak-eyed look was always in need of just such bucking up.

Linda said, "What do you think Astrid? Don't you think the boys did well tonight?"

Like two mothers who'd just come from watching the school play performed.

Linda said, "Nicky thinks it was a good night."

"Rather ordinary," said Astrid turning up her nose. For her the one really good show had been in Chicago.

The Mayor of Mobile spoke like he had a mouthful of spoon bread, and when he handed his fair city's key to Bill Wyman the Englishman stared at his shoes and went quickly off to sign release forms and contracts that had been flown up a few minutes earlier from the lawyers in New York.

Uptight

In Mobile, two young men were dragged out of the hall by the hair by local police when they attempted to climb onto the stage, and on the plane ride home to New Orleans afterwards Security Chief Stanley Moore told me how much he enjoyed briefing cracker police chiefs on how to handle young people when they come to a Stones performance.

Stanley said, "Some of those cats haven't changed a bit. They're cracker through and through. You ought to see the look on their faces when I come into the hall, me being as I am, and I tell them let the kids have a good time and I don't want no rough stuff. For God's sakes you'd think they would know better by now, but some don't."

Stanley is a strong, bitter, capable, dapper man, with a hand brocaded with the marks of much hard labor, and a cold eye for social fact. He is his own Main Man—tough, though not a bully.

"I'm having a ball with these crackers," he said, but told me he would be glad when we were out of the Deep South. Then he had to go up front to speak to Peter Rudge about security in Tuscaloosa.

"What do you know about Tuscaloosa?" Bill Wyman asked me.

"It's a University town . . ."

"Frankly I don't think they're in session now," Bill said. We played there once before. It's not too far from Birmingham." He pronounced it in the manner of the English. Bill was unwinding slowly, as if stretching himself out into the darkness of the aisle to a fullness of size, actually elongating himself.

"I'll tell you about the last time we played Tuscaloosa," Bill said. "It was only a few years ago, but most of the kids still had short hair, and the most far out thing was when the Dean's office announced on the PA that curfew hour was being extended beyond midnight."

We shared one of Bill's half-and-half butts and our bellies swelled out softly against the safety belts.

Presently Bill unfastened himself and began to talk. He told me about his Tudor mansion in the English countryside. "It has a moat and a drawbridge," Bill said.

He told me how much he loved animals. He has numerous pets: dogs, cats, birds, cattle—a regular Noah's ark.

Bill must have been feeling somewhat homesick because he spoke next about his son. Bill explained he had custody because "the boy's mother wasn't that interested in him."

"My boy's in school now," Bill said, "but he'll be over later. He'll meet us in New York."

He drew wistfully on the butt and his face tightened, and he stared down into the hazy squash of light of a small Southern city that we were now passing over. Bill produced no photos from his wallet; we did not exchange addresses and telephone numbers; but it was as if we had. We were like a couple of commercial travelers returning home after a hard sell through the Midlands. It would presently be time for high tea. Meantime the task

Uptight

was to make ourselves comfortable.

The American South is a great well of authenticity into which English musicians like the Stones feel they must occasionally dip their bejewelled fingers to come away aware and refreshed. It's the heartland of rhythm and blues, and it holds a special place in their fantasy lives similar to that which the caves at Qumran or the Wilderness of Zin has for biblical scholars. That is why the Stones called their album *Exile on Main Street*. It is that text from popular folk experience that they gloss again and again, and if they were willing to play auditoriums in Mobile and Tuscaloosa and pass up the large open-air concerts that they might have booked elsewhere it is because they wished somehow to bring on the rush of the antique and funky. But every new Southern auditorium looks alike; from Dallas to Chattanooga it's late Lincoln Center glass and concrete poured out like cubes of sugar, or glazed donuts. The Stones had hoped to get turned on in the South. They were probably just a little bit disappointed.

Hemmed in on all sides by security, wrapped in plastic, and hatched out every night by Rudge and his advance men inside these big glass goose eggs, the Stones were succumbing to their own inner tediums. The tour ran smoothly, despite minor incidents. At six in the afternoon you woke up for breakfast, were briefed by Rudge, answered a few phone messages, turned on, and went off to the new hall, where you waited about and munched canapes, and entertained well-wishers, or spoke to the girlfriend of

the local promoter, or got turned on to a new guitar, or a fancy
new embroidered jacket that some peddler had managed to bring
backstage. Always you performed to enthusiastic crowds who
were sometimes more or less spaced. Then you ran back into the
camper, and either went off by plane to another new city, or
dined somewhere in a large party at an expensive and
uninteresting restaurant, and then, after maybe partying through
half the night, you fell off into a drugged sleep to begin the new
day at twilight, all over again.

By the time we reached Tuscaloosa the Stones had been on the
road for nearly a month; Jagger's cake walk had turned into a
reeling spin; he was like a satellite that could never quite get off
course, and if it was an effort for him to bear up and smile all the
time, and appear contemptuously amiable, it was also a wonder to
me how he managed never to vary the range of his frowns and
smiles. He never looked weary or down, never jowled up, or
bagged under the eyes; it was as if he got up every morning and
stretched a fine new mask of skin across his face.

But by Tuscaloosa most of the talk was about the July 4th
weekend hiatus that was forthcoming. Some would be going to St.
Thomas; others to New York. It had the feeling of a bunch of
kids at camp singing "Two more days of vacation/then we go to
the station/back to civilization/the train will carry us home . . ."

The Stones wouldn't ever say they were hurting, but they
probably were. Jagger's concentration, which is more noteworthy

Uptight

than his grace, was off. Now he sometimes looked like a well-rehearsed Raggedy Andy doll, a puppet jerked on strings, and only occasionally was he able to flash on his brother Keith in a performance, or on Charley, or on Mick Taylor; and Nicky Hopkins looked like he had gotten lost somewhere inside the caves of his own eye sockets.

A heavy somnolence, halfway to euphoria, had fallen over everybody on the tour. Only the rote necessity to seem up for each concert roused them from it. The Stones got cross with their friends when they fucked up, and aboard the plane people dealt with each other with that sort of quiet civility that is the way despair is sometimes carefully covered over and concealed.

After the Tuscaloosa concert Mick Taylor said he felt they had all played well together, but Nicky Hopkins said, "I couldn't hear a thing."

For once, in Tuscaloosa, our orbital flight was nearly short-circuited. The Stones left the hall in their usual afterglow of speeded up limos, but when the bus with the crew and the press tried to get out of the parking lot we were engulfed by a massive wall of people, cops, and cars.

The plane was five miles off, at a tiny country airport. We poked our way through the flood slowly, with Peter Rudge just about to blow his kugel.

Then the driver meekly announced he thought he had a flat

rear tire and Rudge really went off against the back of the guy's neck.

"KEEP DRIVING. I DON'T GIVE A DAMN WHAT HAPPENS TO YOUR BUS. IT'S GOT TO BE YOUR FAULT, AND WE CAN'T AFFORD TO SIT AROUND WHILE YOU CHANGE TIRES. KEEP DRIVING. YOU'LL GET THERE. WE HIRED YOU TO DO A JOB FOR US," Peter shouted, turning up the treble knob to *NASTY* every time the redneck started to complain.

We were limping along the shoulder of the road on a piece of rim and five pounds of shredded rubber.

"Hey mister please," the driver pleaded.

Rudge said, "YOU JUST GET US THERE. THERE'S NO EXCUSE FOR THIS. WE'RE PAYING YOU FOR GOOD SERVICE. ALL IT COSTS YOU IS A LITTLE TIME, BUT IT'S COSTING US THOUSANDS . . ."

He was becoming ulcerous and Joe Bergman dragged him away and had him sit down with her and the luggagemaster, Rock 'n Roll Producer Franky Barcelona's driver, Willy, was ordered to keep bullying the driver, to give him little verbal jabs, and pokes, and *shtupps* until we were, finally, at the airport.

By now we were riding on just one steel guitar string and a stink of burning rubber, almost like a hovercraft. Pleading imminent danger, the driver pulled into a gas station next to a roadhouse.

Uptight

The crew sprang to action stations: Some were posted to call the plane and brief them on the situation; others were sent out on sapping duty to the roadhouse to request rides from people at the bar. Surprisingly, these were quickly forthcoming.

Shell-shocked by the sudden blitz of limey crewmen, black bodyguards, zonked-out hairies, and ladies in muumuus, the gas station attendant stood and stared at us, vaguely, and gave the key to the Men's Room to the bus driver when he asked for change of ten dollars.

So much sudden frantic activity around the gas pumps also roused everybody else, momentarily, from their comas, as if this breakdown in the smooth running of the machine was just the sort of chaos people needed to remember that they were not so much freight, but sentient beings.

The first volunteer driver from the bar appeared. Like a captain on the bridge of a drowning ship, Rudge hollered into the windows of the bus. "Rolling Stones women first, then media women . . ."

"Talk about male chauvinism," somebody observed.

Peter glared at us, much too busy to air his contempt for such ill-advised banalities.

We pushed our ways aboard various commandeered vehicles like French doughboys on the way to Verdun, and drove at such breakneck speeds to the waiting plane that one of the cars in our procession almost drove right into the sucking engine of the already whirring jet. Leroy screamed from the doorway at the youngish blonde matron who drove, and she blanched, as if caught in an act of adultery, or miscegenation, backed away with a screech, and released her passengers without anybody even saying thank you.

At the Sheraton Hotel in Nashville at three that same morning great confusion prevailed about room assignments and reservations, and there was much delay. One of the Stones's lady friends was angry. She could not remember the phony name under which Keith was registered. Was it Count Ziggenpuss?

Half an hour later we have all reassembled in an over-decorated, darkly Italianate restaurant of the *Mezzogiorno,* drinking vintage wines, and ordering elaborate indigestible meals.

For me this was the last supper; I would be leaving the tour after the concert the next day. Jagger sat at one end of a long collection of tables in the shape of a cross, bathed in his customary halo of confidence and smarts. His dinner companions were Charley Watts and Mick Taylor. The apostle Nicky Hopkins sat with his girl at the T-bar of the cross, among the press. It was four thirty before the loaves and fishes began to appear. In a low, carefully modulated voice Mick discussed future recording plans with his two buddies.

Enter one chubby, balding, rather inept Eyetalian violinist of the sort who strolls from table to table while the *maître de* in his Mafioso-blue tuxedo takes orders, and who does he choose to pick

Uptight

Ethan A. Russell

on with his inept scrapings and fiddlings—Mick the Jagger.

The man has a whole repertoire of *can't dos*. He can't play Country or Blue Grass music, can't remember melodies, though he plays by ear, and can only just barely get through *'O Sole Mio,* and thinks he should like to serenade Mick with "Ruby Tuesday." Exactly the sort of *chutzpah,* one might assume, to bring on a Jagger rush, a temper tantrum; in fact it elicited a fit of sudden tolerance from poor Mick.

He wished to be helpful. He tried to seem amused. He even made requests which were all scraped at with a timid faltering *brio* of ineptitude and then discarded in favor of another work from the Stones's repertoire.

Jagger decided to concentrate on talking to his friends, and the man would not let him alone. He simply would not relent. He was persistent, and looked as if he'd been egged on by some wiseacre-ish well-wisher in our crowd to really get Mick's goat.

That sort of sadism is real and not camped up, as in *Midnight Rambler*, and Jagger, with all the love for his fellow men he could possibly bring forward, had just had about enough of earache for one evening.

He stretched out one hand, as if to place a papal malediction, and then his long thin finger pointed at the air above the man's baldpate, accusingly, as if he was instructing a music pupil who had failed to prepare the lesson well, and the finger wobbled from side to side, like a metronome bar that has come unsprung.

Rapt, and intent, the Sicilian Candidate tried to keep time to Mick's beat. He honestly thought they were just jamming together, and they were, to a theme of humiliation.

For, abruptly, a rich dramatic hillbilly erupted from Jagger's pursing lips and seemed to hang in the heavy air like ectoplasm

Uptight

from the grave of the late Hank Williams:

> "I spoke not a word
> Though it meant my life
> For I'd been in the arms
> Of my best friend's wife . . ."

The put-on left the man blushing. He'd gotten the message: You dummy! You rude bullying oaf. You're shit, and I don't want you to bother me, and my friends. You hear?

The violinist ran for cover, like an Italian General at Tobruk.

"That's it . . . that's the first real moment on this tour," said Robert Frank, who sat next to me. He was pissed that he hadn't brought his camera.

Jagger sang on:

> "*Nobody knows . . .*
> *Nobody knows . . .*"

He seemed to wish to goad the man further into his catatonia of self-loathing. But, then he broke it off like the stem of a wine glass between his fingers, and turned to Charley and started talking about recording again, like a debutante turns to her partner in bed after having just scolded the maid for not knocking.

The mood switch was so sudden that it seemed as if Mick couldn't have been that angry to be laughing now, in such an off-hand, light-textured way. But the man, after all, was just a servant; he would recover and next time he would know how to behave toward his betters.

Ethan Russel served me a glass of his twelve-dollar wine.

"One word is worth a thousand pictures," I told Ethan.

He and Frank smiled back at me, severely.

At five-thirty the following afternoon I went down to the hall in Nashville to check out a rumor about counterfeit tickets and perhaps talk to Chipmonck and some of the advance men.

It was pleasantly warm in Nashville, mountain air, with a touch of birdsong, and the breezes warbling warmly. The town's many public buildings wore a freshly-washed grey look, and the women out shopping wore Fifties print dresses with matching white shoes and handbags.

A large station wagon arrived just as I did at the auditorium. Out of it were poured two or three rosy-cheeked chubby country girls, a few bushy-haired members of the Stevey Wonder band, and Keith, entirely bedraggled though somehow seeming very pleased to see me again and greet me.

He must have sensed he had seemed scary to me, at times, during the tour, for now he took me gently around the shoulder and led me with him into the hall.

He looked calm and relaxed. His death-like pallor and sunken

Uptight

cheeks and frosty thatch of hair were all bathed inside a warm wash of good feeling, and his body seemed much less tight and spastic.

"Hi Richard, how are you?" he asked, as if we'd somehow become acquainted during the tour in ways I did not know of. His smile and welcome seemed genuine enough; it was that of a man who'd just gotten off, as if he'd either smoked or fucked everything within ten miles of Tuscaloosa during the last eighteen hours, and now that his appetite was finally sated and glutted he wanted us to have a friendly chat.

I asked where he'd been.

Keith explained he had stayed overnight in Tuscaloosa to party with the Stevey Wonder band and they'd had a ball, in his words, "fucking and sucking."

A stout, agile trumpeter with a bebop goatee grabbed Keith from behind, around the waist, and hugged him tenderly: "Beautiful man . . ."

"Hey man, you're really beautiful, do you know that?"

I think this pleased Keith a little. I could feel him softening. He wasn't used to being called beautiful, and he was shy.

"You know how it is," he said to me, "if you're traveling on a tour like this you have to get together with them sometime."

"Sounds like a lot of fun," I said. "I'm sorry I wasn't invited . . ."

"Sorry Richard," he said, touching me on the wrist, "this was just something between us musicians. You understand . . ."

"Sure!"

We were holding hands in the dressing room together; Keith, with his ruined old face and the one earring and the pirate's grin seemed to be clutching just as much as me. He squeezed my hand and I squeezed his, and we saw each other briefly, then. We were just two different styles of scaredy-cat. He'd gone one way and I another, but that didn't mean we couldn't be together for a little while. We didn't have to be scared of each other. He was a professional, in pain, yes, but he meant me no harm. He hurt too much himself.

"Come and see me when you get to New York," I told Keith. He said "Of course."

He took my name and address and telephone number.

He seemed to wish to assure me that he felt warmly toward me, but that he was also this really big freak. Folding the slip of paper into his breast pocket, he said, "Goodbye Richard. Take care of yourself."

It was so soft, it was almost motherly, and just a little sad, as if he did not know when he might be departing from this vale of tears for good.

The wasted look came over his face again. I thought he must be dying and I was very sad and looked away and went about my own business, fast.

Uptight

Later

Mick Jagger is Mr. Peanut: a black top hat; a Preparation-H smile.

His style is to Rock 'n Roll what sick humor is to comedy: an active repudiation of the joyful experience it purports to be about.

A Bob Dylan can be openly sentimental, or angry, or both, as can John Lennon. Never Jagger. He is much too contemptuous of himself to allow these moods to be played out straight. Always just stepping backwards out of his reeling body and grimacing face to look at himself and sneer—at himself, at all those who see him as really being into something, such as experience. Its not so much the mood of the street fighter as of the lower-middle-class wise guy, self-deprecating and schizoid, desperately the bourgeouis no matter how much he may try to shock.

And wherever such a type is found there are apt to be certain victims, stoics who con themselves into believing they are of less value than this other person. It is a sort of collaboration of aliens, of enemies; Jagger plays Tom Sawyer to Keith Richards' Huck Finn.

Poor uptight, bedraggled Keith is hag-ridden, haunted, yet somehow available; he lends a lyric spirit to the Stones. In years to come one can imagine Mick as an MP from Soho, a successful movie person, or an international high-lifer. Keith is a Stone, a musician; he will probably always be one, uncommunicative, though instinct with feeling; hostile, fearful, though never quite so contemptuous as his old chum Mick. It's his self-destructiveness

Uptight

Wendi Lombardi

that gives the Stones their unique *éclat*. Always to have this crazy little kid you can two-step around. The crazy little kid tries to express his feeling and you go "gurgle gurgle gurgle."

You say, "There, you see. He can't help himself. But don't worry yourself sick one bit. I'll get somebody else to look after him, if I can't," and then of course you don't, because, after all, it's Keith's thing and who has so much time.

The spirit of our age is cost efficiency; the Stones are a sort of animated time-motion study. To reduce music to rage is to reduce intimacy to fucking, a statement that is true enough insofar as it goes, though not very interesting. Remember the days, gentle reader, when everybody was just a little bit fatter and Rock was *Maybelline* or Elvis, and noise was not necessarily synonymous with energy. The wall-to-wall publicity, the squalor of dead talents, lives emptied out like swill buckets, seemed to demand that the sound level be raised higher and higher to a silent, ear-piercing screech, as if to cauterize that stinking ear infection, to stop it up at once with a big ball of grey cotton wool noise.

The Stones were around for all that, trying to make contact somehow, and finally declaring that it was irrelevant, or impossible, or both. They were trying to turn black into white, to come in colors, to call their numbness feeling, and their feeling numbness. It was a sort of reductionist boast: every human being was essentially beautiful; that way you never really had to look very hard at anybody. Beating up was a way of making contact;

that way you never had to know, or be with, anybody. And a somewhat callow notion of human evil went the rounds that was simply disruptive and bullying of the real push which humankind has been making from the beginning of Time: to become more human, and alive.

The chief stimulant of Rock Culture is not drugs, but organically produced adrenalin—more of a hype than a high. You flash a moment or two, and that ends that.

Let us go then, you and I, to New York City, adrenalin capital of the world, some three weeks after the events which I have recorded as transpiring in the American South with the Stones, to the roof of the St. Regis Hotel for a birthday party for Mick Jagger. The wealthy hosts are Mr. and Mrs. Ahmed Ertigan of Atlantic Records. The guests include Andy Warhol, Marjoe, Jack Paar, Zsa Zsa Gabor, and Charley Watts's toddler. Its three in the morning. Muddy Waters's Chicago Blues Band has been alternating sets with the Count Basie orchestra. It is rumored they will be playing until well past dawn. There has been generous food and drink, a crush over invitations, at least two large birthday cakes for Mick and a small stuffed panda present from Bianca; apparently, nobody has given any thought to hiring any nursemaids or babysitters. Presumably, existentialists do not need baby sitters. The elegantly attired Stones' kids rub their tired red eyes; they collapse across resentful maternal and paternal laps. It doesn't feel very different from the relative parties I used to go

to in the old days with my parents: hostile strangers everywhere, adults, boredom, fatigue, chatter, though *these* little bundles of rage are dressed in *boutiquey* Mother Hubbards or ruffled tunics, with Lord Fauntleroy bangs, and shiny avocado rinses.

I had not seen any of the Stones in three weeks and I was eager to make eye contact with some of them, perhaps Charley, or Keith, but the crowd around their ringside tables was far too pressing, and the wasted looks on all their faces demanded distance.

Nobody seemed to be having much fun at this party; Mick and Bianca seemed cross with each other; I wanted to be with my two old chums and knew I could not.

Standing next to my date, holding hands, near the dance floor, I came upon Mick Taylor. He was without a date, and for once seemed glad to see me. He seemed to want to talk.

"How are you, Richard?" he asked in that concerned tone of voice that is sometimes used by doctors of medicine when inquiring about the health of their most gravely ill patients.

I told Taylor I was in reasonably good spirits and we shook hands, and grocked each other, once, briefly.

"Parties are difficult for me," I said. "It's a pity we never had a chance to talk before this on the tour . . ."

Taylor allowed that he was in agreement with the perception.

I said, "I really liked hearing you play."

Taylor expressed his gratitude.

I asked if he was enjoying the party.

"Not too much! What about you?"

"It's kind of interesting . . ."

"Yes," he said, "you would be."

We were both so alone, then, it didn't really seem to matter that I had a date and he didn't. Having only your loneliness to share with another person is a loser's bit. It feels so cold and wet and sort of dead.

The party was now in full swing; a few rather pretty drag queens and some straight-married couples were jouncing back and forth on the dance floor.

Taylor was also looking away. He said, "See you, Richard . . ."

I said, "See you again sometime . . ."

Our faces never once softened. We had perfect party manners. This was, after all, a celebration: the Stones had just completed their most financially successful tour of America *ever,* without any serious incidents, save one. Now they were going off to be with themselves, for a while, and Mick had reached beyond the age of thirty on behalf of Ahmed Ertigan and Atlantic Records, and with the help of a little smack for his friends—for which he would later be busted.

I am thirty-eight.

Some people really do believe Time is Love.

Uptight